The Cost

The Cost

A Business Novel to Help Companies Increase Revenues and Profits

Chris Domanski

BEP

BUSINESS EXPERT PRESS

Leader in applied, concise business books

The Cost: A Business Novel to Help Companies Increase Revenues and Profits

Copyright © Business Expert Press, LLC, 2021.

Interior design by Exeter Premedia Services Private Ltd., Chennai, India

First published in 2021 by
Business Expert Press, LLC
222 East 46th Street, New York, NY 10017
www.businessexpertpress.com

ISBN-13: 978-1-95334-934-7 (paperback)
ISBN-13: 978-1-95334-935-4 (e-book)

Business Expert Press Supply and Operations Management Collection

Collection ISSN: 2156-8189 (print)
Collection ISSN: 2156-8200 (electronic)

First edition: 2021

10 9 8 7 6 5 4 3 2 1

Printed in the United States of America.

To curiosity, the biggest gift and curse of my life.
To my wife, Angie, for her help and support.
To Doug T. Hicks, Jeff Miller, Nazire Yaman, and
Leonard and Julie Magro for their feedback.

Description

The Cost is a story of a cost engineering consultant named Doug Benson who does his best to help companies understand and improve cost. When Doug arrives at Electronica, the company is on a verge of bankruptcy and hardly even knows why. He must use all his cost engineering knowledge and leadership skills amidst some considerable corporate drama all the while fighting his own personal demons in order to give Electronica a chance. The type of situations that he finds himself in are happening all over the world every day and the results are often dramatic with people losing jobs, stakeholders losing millions of dollars, and communities losing hope.

The Cost aims to describe a cost engineering process and expose the many things that can go wrong with it. Although the story and characters are fictional, the events are based on real occurrences. If these seem familiar to the reader, it is probably because they happen daily across thousands of global companies in many different manufacturing industries. Making money is not always straight forward. Having a great product that people want usually helps, but understanding your own cost is critical to success for most companies. Unfortunately, it is much too often that companies do not understand their own cost, which leads to lost opportunities to win business and to make money. In most severe cases, lack of cost engineering capability or its misuse can lead to failed businesses.

The Cost demonstrates various cost engineering methodologies and tools. Starting with the concepts of cost estimating, which is a necessary navigational tool for a cost engineer, to cost controlling and to various cost optimization tools, such as cost reduction workshop and gap analysis, cost engineering requires a spectrum of activities to assure the lowest possible cost. The cost engineering process requires disciplined control throughout the product development process and throughout the complete life cycle of a product. Gate reviews during product's development are common for many companies, but cost optimization efforts should also be part of the process. It is too late to start those activities only after the design is finalized, or worse, after the tools are built. Cost optimization must take place as early as the concept design. It is not enough to build a product that works, it must also cost only as much as the price and profit requirements dictate.

The Cost is not only for those in the cost engineering field. This book is for everyone that is in a manufacturing business or any other kind of business for that matter. It is for engineers, buyers, sales reps, accountants, operations folks, and business consultants. This book is also for anyone that is leading a business and has the power to employ cost engineering to make their company successful. If you are a CEO, or a COO, or a General Manager, please stop and consider whether you truly understand your cost and ask yourself if you are doing everything in your power to optimize it. Give those in your organization that fight daily to understand and improve cost the respect that they deserve. Acknowledge, promote, and pay them just like everyone else.

Keywords

costing; cost engineering; cost estimating; should costing; target costing; cost-based negotiation; cost allocation; cost analytics; profitability analysis; cost reduction; cost optimization; cost controlling; gap analysis; quoting; VA/VE; business objectives; business transformation; bankruptcy; business novel; business case studies; product development; supplier collaboration; business consulting; corporate drama; corporate development; business development; business

Contents

Preface

If profit is a difference between sales and cost, then why are there thousands of business books about increasing sales and very few about decreasing cost? While sales is associated with fancy designer suits, golf, speed boats, and sports cars, the thought of cost conjures images of nerdy accountants somewhere in a basement of an old office building. Yet, both are just as important in that simple equation that results in profit.

If you are a cost estimator, or a cost controller, or a cost optimization specialist, I have a feeling that you, at some point of your career, felt marginalized or unappreciated by your company. While you saw the huge impact that you were making to the company's bottom line, others might have seen you only as a noncore function of the organization. While Engineering, Purchasing, or Operations enjoyed growth and job security, you wondered when your promotion will come or whether you will have a job tomorrow.

If this sounds to you like a disgruntled corporate employee complaining about his career, then you would be wrong. What bothers me is simply inefficiency, that is all. I tell people that I am allergic to it, because inefficiency, waste, and nonvalue work make me mad. This is why, I am bothered by an inefficient approach to cost by so many companies. It is because they can do so much better. It bothers me even more when people lose jobs because their companies do not know or focus on cost.

The Cost is a story of a cost engineering consultant named Doug Benson who, like me and many others in this field, does his best to help companies understand and improve cost. When he arrives at Electronica, the company is on a verge of bankruptcy and hardly even knows why. He must use all his cost engineering knowledge and leadership skills amidst some considerable corporate drama, all the while fighting his own personal demons in order to give Electronica a chance. The type of situations that he finds himself in are happening all over the world every day, and the results are often as dramatic, with people losing jobs, stakeholders losing millions of dollars, and communities losing hope.

While my first book, *Cost Engineering: A Practical Method for Sustainable Profit Generation in Manufacturing*, serves as a technical manual, *The Cost* shows cost engineering concepts in real-life action. Although neither book is able to capture the full scope of cost engineering methodologies on their own, the two books combined hope to achieve just that.

The Cost is not only for those in the cost engineering field and not only to make them feel better about their work. This book is for everyone who is in a manufacturing business or any other kind of business for that matter. It is for engineers, buyers, sales reps, accountants, operations folks, and business consultants. This book is also for anyone who is leading a business and has the power to employ cost engineering to make their company successful. If you are a CEO, CFO, COO, CPO, or a general manager, please stop and consider whether you truly understand your cost and ask yourself if you are doing everything in your power to optimize it. Give those in your organization who fight daily to understand and improve cost the respect that they deserve. Acknowledge, promote, and pay them just like everyone else. They love sports cars too.

CHAPTER 1

The Problem

Monday, Day 1 of 28

I was invited to join an executive-level meeting the same day I walked into Electronica's building for the first time. All I knew about Electronica was that it was a medium-sized company headquartered just outside of metro Detroit with factories in the United States, Mexico, China, and Poland. I also knew that there was probably a good reason why I was here. Electronica's CEO, Bill Rasor, insisted that I attend the meeting and essentially pushed me into the conference room where everyone else was already gathered. My entrance was met with sudden silence and suspicious eyes of about 10 individuals. The sea of designer suits should have made me feel intimated, but this was not my first rodeo. I wore an old tweed suit jacket for this exact purpose. Even though I was only 49 and looked closer to 40 because I exercised and took care of myself, the jacket gave me the look of a tenured professor that took everyone back to their college days and gave a proper measure of intimidation. To put a final touch on it, I had inserted my University of Michigan pin into the lapel of the jacket, which seemed to imply that maybe I was someone important or at least that I had some brains.

"Let's get right to it, gentlemen," said Rasor before anyone could introduce themselves to me. He sat in a luxury leather chair at the top of the long mahogany table, and the sea of suits quickly got into their chairs. He was a tall man with a demeanor of a dictator, so it looked like he was sitting at a throne even though he had a table in front of him. There were no chairs left at the table, so I sat in one of the chairs along the wall. If I was not an outsider before, I sure felt like one now.

"So?" continued Rasor. "What is Volta's response to our last quote?"

A handsome dark-haired man spoke up right away seemingly anxious to grab the spotlight from Rasor. "They don't think we're competitive."

A wave of sighs rose up from the room. The luxury leather chairs started to swing from side to side as people nervously looked around the room. Volta Motors was the largest electric car and truck manufacturer in the world, with over eight million vehicles sold annually, and it seemed Electronica's future was on the line.

"Damn it!" shouted Rasor. "Why the hell not?"

"Bill," spoke the handsome man again, "as I said before, our previous quote was thirty percent off Volta's target and I asked the team here to sharpen their pencils, but our latest quote is still twenty percent too high. I think their target is real, so I can't sweet talk Volta into giving us the business unless I get better numbers from everyone."

So, that establishes the corporate culture I will be dealing with; shed the blame and point the finger at everyone else. Not unusual in the high-stakes business like this, but it will make my job more difficult. It will be tough to get the truth out of people. I took out my notebook and wrote down.

"ISSUE #1: Sharpening pencils to get to the numbers"

"What happened, George? I thought you squeezed the cost out of every bucket?" asked Rasor of a nerdy looking man sitting next to him. The man's body seemed like it would be more comfortable in a laboratory frock than the designer suit he was wearing. Or, maybe he was just not comfortable with the question.

"I did, Bill," said George, "but our plant won't budge any further on new investment or processing cost and purchasing said that we can't squeeze more out of the supplier quotes, so there's not much more I can do. I already lowered our profit down to six percent. Anything below that would have to go to the board of directors for approval."

Here we go with some more deflection and finger pointing, I thought. Shit rolls downhill, I wonder who the plants and purchasing are going to blame. My answer came quickly.

"If engineering could design a product that is common with our current products, then I wouldn't need new machines!" shouted a heavy-set man who probably represented manufacturing.

"Or smaller and less complex parts. I'm already buying at the lowest prices that I can," said another short man with a Spanish accent, obviously representing purchasing.

"That's enough!" shouted Rasor before any more fingers can be pointed. "Let me remind you again that if we don't win this business, we are finished."

Rasor let the word *finished* hang in the air before continuing. "We haven't won any business in two years. Our capacity utilization is down to fifty percent. Our profit is down to two percent. Our cash flow is almost nothing. How long do you think we have before some changes are made around here?" Nobody dared to answer this question. All the heads were hung low avoiding eye contact with Rasor. "I'll tell you how long. The final round of quotes is due to Volta in four weeks. You have exactly that long to turn this around, because if we don't win this business, then there's nothing else and we might as well close the doors."

Rasor stood up and walked over to the nearby refrigerator built into a small butler's pantry. The silence hung in the room as he poured himself a ginger ale. He pulled something from the inside pocket of his suit jacket, but he turned his back to everyone, so I could not tell what it was. Whatever it was, he hung it over his glass then put it back into his suit jacket. I guessed it was some sort of fire water, and I could have used some myself as Rasor walked over to me.

"What do you think, Doug?" he said to me. "What is our problem?"

The luxury leather chairs swung toward me, and I felt daggers flying at me from the suits. I was stunned by Rasor's questions, and so, I just stared at everyone while trying to formulate an appropriate answer. I felt stupid for not having a quick and witty response. Fortunately, Rasor gave me more time by breaking up the awkward silence.

"Sorry, I apologize. Where are my manners? Everyone, this is Doug Benson. Doug is a consultant friend of our board and he will be working with us to figure this thing out."

There was no applause. Not even a head nod or smile to welcome me. Instead, the awkward silence got more awkward. I have been consulting for over five years and was used to chilly receptions, but this was the coldest and most awkward one I have ever gotten. I could not wait to call my buddy, Jim Miller, to thank him for getting me into this mess. Jim was my roommate at the University of Michigan, and we have been close friends since then, but I suddenly felt an urge to end that friendship for twisting my arm to help him with Electronica. I did owe Jim for helping me in my career, he called in some favors to get me a vice president (VP) job once at a company that I used to work for, but mister fancy board member did not tell me that he is throwing me into a den of angry wolves.

"Thanks for having me, Bill," I finally said. "Obviously, it's too soon for me to have an opinion," I lied. "But, I'm looking forward to working with all of you in the next coming weeks and the impressive talent in this room will, I'm sure, be able to get to the bottom of it."

It was my standard practice to stroke everyone's egos. I found that pretty much everyone, without exception, loved to hear how great they were. I also wanted to make sure they knew that it was not going to be just me trying to figure this out, we would all have to do it as a team.

"Perfect!" exclaimed Rasor, unconvincingly. "Let's get on with it then!"

Tuesday, Day 2 of 28

I woke up the next day with a bit of a headache. I knew myself well and knew that my brain was already trying to figure out how to deal with my new project while I was sleeping. At least the hotel I was staying in had a comfortable bed. I turned on the TV to keep me company. It did not take me long to shower, dress, eat a breakfast bar, chase Motrin with some coffee, and get on the road.

I was met in Electronica's front lobby by Emily, the CEO's administrative assistant. She was an attractive woman, probably in her early 40s, with large brown eyes and long black hair. I was a bit stunned by her, and I do not even remember if she said anything to me or if I responded. She gestured to me, and I followed her up the stairs.

"How are you?" I exulted finally, trying to be as friendly as possible, knowing that administrative assistants pretty much ran every company. If I could get her to be my friend, then I could increase my chances of success. Plus, she was very attractive, and I was single.

"Bill would like you to meet with our VP of Finance, George Sewell," she said dryly.

"Sure, that makes sense," I replied trying not to show my disappointment in the coldness of her response.

George Sewell and his Quoting Manager, Mark Harrington, were already waiting for me in George's vast corner office. While Sewell was probably in his late 50s or early 60s, Harrington was in his mid-40s and athletic. In fact, he looked like a tennis player who accidently put on a suit.

"Ah, fellow U of M alumni," Harrington greeted me, noticing a pin in my lapel. "Hell of a football team we should have this year, don't you think?"

I cannot say that I was a real football fan, but I knew his type well and knew that disagreeing would not endear him to me, so I said, "Yes, I'm looking forward to the season."

"Why don't you tell us how we can help you, Doug," said Sewell as we sat around his small conference table. "And, I apologize, but Mark and I only have half an hour. We have an important month end close meeting that we must attend."

"I thought we had two hours to discuss this topic," I said confused. I knew I would be dodged, but this was fast. I got cut off at the knees before we ever got started.

"Sorry, I wish we had that kind of time. There is some real business that we need to attend to," Sewell said, implying that my work was not a real business. "But, don't worry, our quoting analyst, Evan Kaminski, will be helping you with your research."

Knowing that there was no point fighting it, I decided to get the most out of the half hour. "Well, I appreciate whatever time I can get with you gentlemen, so why don't we get started."

Sewell and Harrington nodded in agreement and smirked to themselves, surely satisfied that they were able to control me and dodge spending a lot of time with me.

"We're ready for your interrogation," said Sewell, and they both chuckled.

"Just a few basic questions, more of a friendly discussion than interrogation," I assured them. An image of water boarding both of them did pass through my mind, though, and gave me a sense of momentary satisfaction. "Let's start at the top, I guess. How do you allocate cost to products?"

Sewell seemed unsure and looked to Harrington.

"Well, we don't allocate to products per se…," stumbled Harrington, "but we have machine rates that define cost per hour, then we multiply by the cycle time that each part spends on that machine. Of course, we multiply by some inefficiency factor for downtime." He stopped there unsure of his answer. "Does that answer your question?"

"Actually, I'm curious about how you measure the cost incurred by any one of your current products. Can you show me a summary of costs for each product that you make today?"

"Sorry, but I'm more focused on period reporting," jumped in Sewell. "I report the costs incurred by our company on a monthly basis. Our company makes car brakes, they are all pretty much the same, just various sizes. So, it doesn't really matter how much each individual product makes."

Sewell stared at me like he was talking to a moron who did not understand most basic things in life. I paused for a second thinking about my next question. "So, Mark, how do you assign fixed overhead costs to products that you're quoting?" I finally said.

"That's easy," launched Harrington as if he just got lucky getting a question he finally knew an answer to. "Plant overhead is already in the machine rates and we apply ten percent on every product for corporate overhead."

"The same ten percent for every product regardless of size or volume?"

"Yes, of course," said Sewell as if he was explaining the concept of two plus two to a five-year-old. "Our SG&A cost was ten percent of sales last year, so that's what our products must incur."

"Very well," I said, but thought the opposite. I wrote in my notebook.

"ISSUE #2: Spread cost evenly on all products, like peanut butter on toast"

"ISSUE #3: Looking into the past instead of the future"

They watched impatiently as I wrote, so I quickly continued. "And how do you calculate your machine rates?"

"Oh, those come from the plant controller." Harrington was happy to point the finger somewhere else.

Sewell's cell phone rang. "Sorry, I have to get this," he said. "Maybe we can pick this up another time?"

"Maybe just one more thing, if you don't mind?" I hurried up. "Can you give me a copy of your quote to Volta?"

Sewell looked uncertain, as if hesitant to provide any evidence, then decided otherwise. "Sure, Mark will get you a summary of the numbers." Then, he picked up the phone and rushed us out of the office with his eyes.

"I have a copy right here actually," said Harrington as we walked out of Sewell's office. He handed me a single sheet of paper (see Table 1.1):

Table 1.1 Volta brake system business case

Inflation/ (Deflation)	Volume ('000)	Year 1 500	Year 2 1,000	Year 3 1,000	Year 4 1,000	Year 5 500		
3%	Raw material	1.20	1.24	1.27	1.31	1.35		
-3%	Purchased parts	90.50	87.79	85.15	82.60	80.12		
	Material, other	0.00	0.00	0.00	0.00	0.00		
3%	Labor	0.83	0.85	0.88	0.91	0.93		
3%	Mfg. overhead	4.15	4.27	4.40	4.53	4.67		
	New investment	1.25	1.25	1.25	1.25	1.25	$5,000	Total ('000)
	Cost of capital	0.28	0.28	0.28	0.28	0.28	$1,125	Total ('000)
2%	Scrap	1.96	1.91	1.86	1.82	1.77		
	Total mfg. cost	100.18	97.60	95.10	92.70	90.38		
	SGA	12.10	11.77	11.41	11.07	10.74		
	SGA ('000)	$6,050	$11,770	$11,410	$11,070	$5,370	$45,670	Total ('000)
	% SGA	10.0%	10.0%	10.0%	10.0%	10.0%	10.0%	Life-time
	Packaging	0.50	0.50	0.50	0.50	0.50		
	Ship/other	1.25	1.25	1.25	1.25	1.25		
	Profit	7.29	6.57	5.89	5.21	4.54		
	% Profit	6.0%	5.6%	5.2%	4.7%	4.2%	5.2%	Life-time
	Profit ('000)	$3,647	$6,565	$5,886	$5,207	$2,268	$23,573	Total ('000)
-3%	Price	121.32	117.68	114.15	110.73	107.40		
	Revenue ('000)	$60,660	$117,680	$114,150	$110,725	$53,702	$456,918	Total ('000)
Year	0	1	2	3	4	5		
Cash flow	($5,000)	$3,178	$5,846	$5,370	$4,895	$2,212		
IRR	81%							
Payback	1.31	years						
5	Years of depreciation							
9%	Borrowing interest rate							
$1,125	Total ('000)							
30%	Tax rate							

Harrington walked me over to a cubicle while I analyzed the numbers. "This is Evan Kaminski, our quote analyst," he said. I looked up and saw a handsome young man in his mid- to late-20s staring at me from his cube. He was quick to jump up with his hand extended.

"Nice to meet you, sir," said Kaminski and actually sounded genuinely pleased to meet me, first person to do so in this company. There was also something else in his eyes. Yes, I was certain now, it was definitely curiosity. Perhaps, I had just met my champion.

"Pleasure is all mine, Evan," I assured him.

"Evan will answer any other questions that you might have," said Harrington. "Also, since George and I are constantly in meetings, our intern, Alex Michaels, will walk you around and introduce you to all the key people in the building."

A head popped up in a cubicle next door. The intern did not look more than 16 years old, and his mop of hair shook nervously as he listened to the conversation. I raised my hand to greet him to be polite, but I was boiling with anger inside. I have not been inside the building for more than an hour, and I was already punted off from the VP all the way down to an intern.

"Thank you for the support," I lied despite my anger. "I look forward to working with all of you."

Harrington rushed back into Sewell's office while I stood there staring at the two young men. It was obvious that neither one of them was given any real direction on what to do with me. They stared back hoping for my direction. When I did not provide one, Kaminski decided to take action. "Why don't we grab you a cubicle. That way you can have somewhere to work."

I settled in two cubicles over from them. It was an empty cube, and the bare walls were a depressing metaphor for this project that I would have to figure out from scratch. I stared at the sheet of paper with the quote summary lying on the table in front of me. Scrubbing 20 percent off of the 121 U.S. dollars price would be a challenge, especially because nobody seemed interested in helping me or helping themselves.

I expected Kaminski to come by and offer help at some point, but when that did not happen, I walked over to his cube. He was staring intently at an Excel spreadsheet on his screen with his fingers tensely hovering over the keyboard as if they were eagle's talons ready to pounce on its prey.

"Working on a quote?" I asked him.

Noticing me just now, he jumped up startled. "Sorry, I'm working on three different quotes at the same time."

"Are you always this busy?"

"Yes, pretty much. I quote about one hundred programs a year and each has at least three or four iterations, so that's between three and four hundred quotes per year."

"That's a lot of wasted quotes considering the company has not won any business in two years." I knew this statement had potential to make him feel bad, but I wanted to see his reaction to it.

Kaminski looked uncomfortable for a second, but recovered quickly to say quietly, "Well, I'm glad you're here actually. I would love to look for solutions to this problem but I'm too busy quoting all the time. I'm looking forward to your findings."

I smiled at him. I was right, this kid will be my champion. Perhaps at this company, with the current culture that it had, his words would make him a trouble maker or a turncoat. However, it is because of this guy and probably others like him that this company still had a chance.

"Good," I said. "I appreciate it and we'll be talking more. In the meantime, I'd like Alex to introduce me to the person responsible for providing you with the purchased parts cost. It's by far the biggest cost bucket, so I'd like to start there."

"Sure. All the supplier quotes are collected by the program purchasing coordinator, Melissa Connors. Alex will take you to meet her." Alex's head popped up again out of his cube as Kaminski spoke.

"Thank you, Evan," I said.

* * *

Alex led me through the sea of uniformly boring beige cubicles, which reminded me why I chose to be a consultant and not to work in one of these corporate prisons. The only inspiration that came from this kind of environment was to get out of it. It was definitely not creativity or action for change. In fact, the uniformity and plainness seemed to say, "Don't rock the boat!"

"Where do you go to school, Alex?" I broke the silence.

"Oakland University," he replied without expanding.

"And what are you studying?"

"Business Administration."

I guess I will have to drag everything out of this kid. "And how do you like working here?"

"I like it very much. It's a great company," he threw out quickly as if it was scripted for an interview.

Alex stopped at one of the cubes occupied by a woman in her mid-30s with short red hair and dressed in a colorful flowery dress that grabbed attention. "This is Melissa," he said, relieved that his task was accomplished and he did not have to answer any more of my questions.

"Hi Melissa, I'm Doug Benson," I explained because Alex clearly was not going to. "I'm a consultant that was hired to help out with the quoting process."

"Great! We need all the help we can get." Connors seemed irritated and obviously was not afraid to speak her mind. Alex seemed frightened of her and scurried away quickly.

"Perfect! That's why I'm here," I reconfirmed just in case she was being sarcastic. "And according to a quote summary I got from Mr. Harrington, purchased parts, at over $90, is the biggest chunk of cost on this Volta business, so I thought I'd speak with you first."

She seemed satisfied with me pointing out that her job was important. "You nailed it on the head. If you could also remind our buyers and suppliers of how important it is, maybe they would get back to me on time with their quotes."

"So, you have to wait for quotes on every part before submitting your totals to the finance team?" I asked.

"Of course, how else would we know how much parts cost?" She looked at me like I was either dumb or trying to trick her somehow.

"Don't you have historical data or a way to estimate the part costs?"

"For some basic parts we do, but three quarters of the BOM is custom to every program. We have a couple of cost estimators to help us, but their numbers are always much lower than what we actually pay, so we can't trust them."

I pondered for a second deciding on how to ask the next question. She looked at her old-fashioned gold-plated watch getting impatient.

"The buyers must have a difficult job trying to negotiate suppliers down," I said finally.

Connors laughed out loud. "Who said that they negotiate anything?" she spat out. "We don't have time to negotiate because we usually have only a couple of weeks to respond with quotes to our customers. But, even if we did have time, the buyers could care less about negotiating with suppliers. Their number one priority is chasing annual savings. They don't have time to worry about quotes for programs that are launching three years from now."

I wrote down in my notebook as she spoke. I also nodded my head during her tirade to make sure I did not offend her by looking down.

"ISSUE #4: Bad objectives drive wrong buyer behavior"

"And how long do suppliers have to reply to requests for quote after designs are finalized?" I continued with the line of questioning.

Connors shook her head in frustration. It was as if I was uncovering the most unpleasant moments in her life. "Our designs are never final, that's one thing. But then I have to scramble and chase suppliers for answers that they are afraid to give because they're not clear what they are quoting. I'm lucky if I have a week to put it all together."

"ISSUE #5: Suppliers sandbagging the numbers"

I wrote and nodded my head faking agreement. "You have been most helpful Melissa. You have a very difficult task indeed."

"It is what it is, we have to quote something," she panned.

"Would you mind sharing a costed BOM with me for the Volta program?" Now that I buttered her up, it was the right time to ask her for favors.

She pulled out a piece of paper from a stack on her table (see Table 1.2). "Here you go. Enjoy!" she said sarcastically as if I was wasting my time.

Table 1.2 Volta brake system costed bill of materials (BOM)

	Piece price	Tooling
ECU housing	$ 20.45	$ 987,000
AL block	$ 8.96	$ -
PCB	$ 6.78	$ -
Connector	$ 5.98	$ 239,000
Capacitors (large)	$ 5.72	$ -
Micro	$ 3.50	$ -
ICs	$ 3.45	$ -
Other (electronic)	$ 15.67	$ -
Other (mechanical)	$ 19.99	$ 345,000
Total	$ 90.50	$ 1,571,000

I studied the piece of paper for a few seconds, then I said, "Perfect! Thank you for all your help. Obviously, you're very busy, so I don't want to take up any more of your time. Perhaps you could do one more thing for me and take me to your cost estimators?"

* * *

I was dropped off in a dark corner of the building with three cubicles separated from the rest of the office floor. This is where the cost estimators sat. As I approached, I noticed three Indian gentlemen occupying the cubes. They looked at me nervously as if I was an Immigration and Customs Enforcement (ICE) officer bringing them bad news. I stopped at the largest cube with a name tag that said "Kumar Ramamurthy."

"Kumar?" I asked without trying to pronounce the last name.

"Yes?" answered a short man with a funny mustache as if he was unsure if he should give up his identity.

"My name is Doug Benson. Melissa said that you are the cost estimating manager?" I did not want to spook him, so I purposely skipped mentioning that I was a consultant working for the CEO.

"That's correct," he said.

"Great. I'm helping her with the quoting process and she said I should talk to you about the great job you're doing with the cost estimates."

"Really?" He seemed shocked but glad to hear a compliment at the same time. I felt bad about the little fib, but I needed to find a way for Kumar to open up to me. "Melissa said that we do a great job?"

I knew it would be hard to believe that Melissa complemented anyone, but he had no way to verify that now. "Maybe you could tell me about how you come up with your estimates?"

Kumar looked me over again, paused on my U of M lapel pin, and then decided to cooperate without asking any questions. Perhaps, he thought that it could not hurt him considering the fact that he was already at the bottom of the hierarchical ladder, at least based on where his cubicle was located.

"Yes, of course," he went on. "It is all based on the design. We get drawings from Engineering and then based on part weights and tolerances we define the manufacturing processes that are needed to make the part. So, if a part is stamped, for example, we figure out the press size needed, the strip layout, the cycle time, the efficiency, and so on. Then, we multiply by different rates and calculate the total manufacturing cost and add standard SG&A and profit percentages to come up with a price."

He watched me nervously as I wrote down in my notebook.

"ISSUE #6: Supplier price estimates are point in time estimates only"

"Great. That's very good." I said and watched his head move from side to side but not in disagreement. "And how do you know what raw material, labor, and overhead rates to apply?"

"We have some historical data from supplier quotes that we use. We usually use the lowest rates just to keep the suppliers honest." He smirked at me as he said the last part.

"So, do you find that your estimates are usually lower than suppliers?"

He flinched a bit when I asked this. I had a feeling that Melissa probably challenged him on this before. He made a clicking sound with his mouth and twisted his body in disagreement. "Suppliers make good money. We can't agree with their pricing."

I wrote in my notebook. "You might be right," I said. "Do you ever negotiate with the suppliers?"

"ISSUE #7: Lack of supplier price validation"

"No, no, no!" he waved his hands as if he did not want to have anything to do with that. "We give our numbers to the buyers and they are supposed to come within ten percent of it. It is their performance objective."

"Interesting. And, on average, how often do they come close to ten percent?"

"Almost always," he said as if it was expected.

I wrote in my notebook again.

"ISSUE #8: Misaligned objectives between functions"

"That's perfect! You did great answering my questions, Kumar. Thank you for all your help."

"You're welcome, sir," he said and smiled wide. "Please let me know if there's anything else I can do for you."

"Maybe just one more thing," I remembered. "If I could have an estimate for the ECU housing on the Volta program that would be great."

"Of course. My best estimator, Navneeth, worked on this one, so it's a very good estimate." He printed a copy of it on his desktop printer and handed it over to me (see Table 1.3).

"Fourteen seventy-eight?" I asked.

"Yes," he answered, not seeing an issue with it.

"That's about thirty percent less than the twenty forty-five price that Purchasing used in the quote to Volta," I pressed him.

He shrugged his shoulders. "I don't control what Purchasing does," he said.

"Very good," I said. "This is exactly what I was looking for."

Table 1.3 ECU housing cost estimate

COST ESTIMATE - BREAKDOWN SHEET

Supplier Name:	Tesung
Program(s):	Volta
Part Number:	NA
Part Description:	ECU Housing
Additional Information:	Navineeth
Prepared by:	

Date:	-
RFQ Number	NA
ECN #:	NA

Total Volume:	10,00,000
Supplier Mfg. Location:	USA
Supplier Shipping Location:	USA
Currency:	Dollar
Exchange Rate:	

Yellow Cells are for Input
Blue Cells are for Output Results

A) RAW MATERIAL:

RAW MATERIAL COST

MATERIAL DESCRIPTION	Raw Material Stock Size (LxWxH)	Gross Material Weight	Net Material Weight	Unit of Measure	Cost/Unit
Copper coil		0.3490	0.6200	kg	$6.66
Resin		0.4000	0.4000	kg	$2.50

	TOTALS

ENGINEERED SCRAP

Gross Raw Material Cost Total	Eng. Scrap Weight	Eng. Scrap Resale Cost/Unit	Eng. Scrap Credit (Eur)
$2.4050	0.1000	$0.7690	$1.0990
$1.2150	0.0400		$0.0100
$3.6200			$1.0990

TOTAL

Total Raw Material Cost:
$1.3550
$1.1750
$2.5380

COST PARETO CHART (% of total)

B) PURCHASED COMPONENTS & MATERIAL:

PURCHASED MATERIAL COSTS

ITEM DESCRIPTION	Supplier Name	Number of Units)	Unit of Measure	Cost/Unit
Pin Plating		1		$0.7500
Blank Plating		1		$1.2500
Epoxy		1		$2.0000
Other		1		$3.1700

TOTAL

Purchased Materials
$0.7500
$1.2500
$2.0000
$3.1700

TOTALS	$7.9700

C) PROCESS COSTS:

PROCESS TIME PER PIECE

PROCESS DESCRIPTION	Part Cycle Time (sec)	Utilization(%)	Pieces Per Cycle	Standard hr/pc	Labour Standard hr/pc
Stamping Pin 1	1.0	90%	1	0.0003	0.0003
Stamping Pin 2	1.0	90%	1	0.0003	0.0003
Stamping Blade 1	1.0	90%	1	0.0003	0.0003
Stamping Blade 2	1.0	90%	2	0.0003	0.0003
Pre-Assembly	44.0	90%	2	0.0055	0.0055
Overmolding	44.0	90%	2	0.0055	0.0055
Final Assembly	44.0	90%	2	0.0055	0.0055

DIRECT LABOR COST

No. of Operators	Base Labour Rate ($/hr)	Labour Cost ($)
1	$20.00	$0.01
1	$20.00	$0.0050
1	$20.00	$0.0050
1	$20.00	$0.0050
1	$20.00	$0.1100
1	$20.00	$0.1100
1	$20.00	$0.1100
TOTALS		$0.3500

OVERHEADS

Hourly OH Rate ($/hr)	OH Cost ($)
$22.00	$0.01
$22.00	$0.0050
$30.00	$0.0050
$30.00	$0.0084
$52.00	$0.2860
$60.00	$0.4070
$80.00	$0.3300
TOTALS	$1.1120

CAPITAL

Hourly Depreciation Rate ($/hr)	Depreciation Cost ($)
$5.00	$0.01
$5.00	$0.0013
$10.00	$0.0025
$10.00	$0.0025
$10.00	$0.1165
$38.00	$0.2960
$38.00	$0.2960
TOTALS	$0.9410

TOTAL COST

Total Labour & OH Cost
$0.0118
$0.0118
$0.0163
$0.0163
$0.4115
$0.7856
$0.6409
$2.0020

D) LOGISTICS, PACKAGING & AMORTISATION:

Cost Type	Description		Cost / Piece
FREIGHT	Cost %	4.0%	0.4663
PACKAGING	Cost %	1.0%	0.1221
DUTY & WAREHOUSE	Cost %	1.0%	0.1221
TOOLING AMORTIZATION	Interest %	9.8%	0.1316
TOOLING ASSET	Cost %	2.0%	0.2442
TOTALS			1.1084

TOTAL COST

MANUFACTURING COST (A+B+C)	$12.7980
FREIGHT, PACK, AMORTISATIONS	$1.1084
Scrap	2.0%	$0.2442
SG&A	4.0%	$0.2426
Profit %	4.0%	$0.4083

TARGET PRICE	$14.7814

% of Total

RAW MATERIAL	17.1%
PURCHASED PARTS	53.9%
LABOUR & OVERHEAD	13.5%
SCRAP	1.7%
AMORTIZATION	9.9%
LOGISTICS & PACKAGING	5.0%
SG&A	5.0%
PROFIT	3.3%

Wednesday, Day 3 of 28

I slept well and took my time getting ready the next morning. Things were now coming into focus on this project. Despite the pushback I got from executives, the working-level people have been very helpful. Twenty-eight days was not a lot of time, but I felt confident to be able to provide my recommendations shortly. Then, I could move on to the next project, hopefully with a bit more pleasant atmosphere. Just a thought of walking into the Electronica building, even though not any different from thousands of similar corporate buildings around the country, made me a little bit queasy. It gave me a similar feeling to the one I got every time I drove by the hospital where I got my colonoscopy.

I stopped by a doughnut shop and picked up two dozen before going into the office. Nothing better than sugar and fat to get people to warm up to me. I got a bucket of coffee as well, mostly because I could not drink the prison coffee that they served for free at the office. After only two days, that coffee was burning a hole in my esophagus.

"Good morning, Emily!" I said with sincere excitement upon seeing her again in the front lobby. I was determined to break that ice the size of an iceberg.

She paused to look at me standing there with two boxes of doughnuts and a bucket of coffee. "We need to get you your own badge," she said finally. I was not sure if I should feel encouraged or discouraged by that. On the one hand, she wanted me to have an easier access to the building where she was located. On the other hand, she was very short with me and showed no emotion. Maybe she was just annoyed with picking me up at the lobby.

After dispensing doughnuts and coffee without getting much appreciation from anyone, I had Alex take me over to meet the program engineers.

"Sorry, you'll have to come back some other time," said the first engineer we visited. I tried not to stereotype, but he looked like he just got off the line where they manufacture introverted, flannel wearing, disheveled engineers. He spoke to us without looking away from his computer screen. "We have a quality issue with one of our brake systems and we're all scrambling to fix it."

Alex was anxious to get back to his work, but I had him take me to the next man up. Unfortunately, we got the same story from him and the next two guys we talked to. Nobody seemed to give a hoot about me being a consultant or that I was reporting to the CEO.

"Please take me to the VP of Engineering," I finally told Alex.

"Are you sure?" Alex seemed frightened.

"Yes, I'm sure."

"He's very busy. I've been here for three months and I've never seen him come out of his office," he said as we walked over to a corner office.

We were met by an admin who gave out that strict librarian vibe, and I immediately lowered my tone of voice while giving her my spiel about who I was and who I was working for.

"He's not available today," she replied unimpressed.

I peeked over her and into the office through the glass wall. A man in his late 40s was sitting at his desk engaged in a heated discussion with two other men.

"He doesn't have any time at all?" I pushed her.

"No. You'll have to come back on Friday."

I stared at her for a moment, but she seemed unmoved. I was losing the admin charm battle at Electronica.

* * *

I spent the rest of the day trying to get someone to help me talk to Engineering, but I did not get anywhere. It seemed the Engineering department did their own thing and cared very little about anything else. It was almost as if it was its own company within a company and had nothing to do with the other functions at Electronica.

I got back to my hotel room, ate a frozen pizza dinner, and tried to watch some TV, but I was seething inside. I was somewhat used to rejection as a consultant, but it was very frustrating working for a company where not a single person wanted me.

I picked up my cell phone and dialed with my speaker on.

"Hello Doug," said Jim Miller on the other side of the line after a few rings. "I'm surprised it took you this long to call me."

"Why are you doing this to me?" I cut to the chase.

Jim laughed. "I'm doing this for you," he said. "You need to get out of your funk."

"I went through a divorce, Jim, but my wife never treated me this badly."

Jim laughed again. "Work will help you move on, buddy."

"You're full of crap. What's wrong with this company?"

"All right, you got me. I really need your help." I knew that he was lying. He was one of the smartest guys I knew, and he could probably figure this out on his own.

"Is it really as bad as I think it is?" I asked. "These guys have their heads so deep inside their asses that they don't even see the cliff in front of them. Not a single executive wants me there, not even the CEO."

"I know, I know. Listen, I might be the only one that wants you there," he admitted.

"Wait, you mean even the board doesn't want me there?" This was worse than I thought.

He cleared his throat. "It's a very delicate situation. This is between you and me, but people have their golden parachutes to think about."

"What!?" I screamed. "You mean they're getting ready for bankruptcy?"

"Hold your horses, Doug. Nobody is talking bankruptcy yet. But, you must understand that if it comes to that, there will be a lot of questions from the creditors. The board and the executive team don't want someone in their office that might point a finger at them."

"Why not just go ahead with the bankruptcy then? It might be easier and cleaner."

Jim stayed silent for a moment, then said, "I'm counting on you, Doug. I really need your help."

That sounded serious. Did Jim have a lot of his own money invested in Electronica? I was assuming that he was just helping them, but maybe he had more at stake.

"You'll have my recommendation, as we agreed," I said finally.

"We'll talk next week," Jim said. "Have a good night, Doug."

"Good night." I hung up the phone.

Well, I guess I had no choice now.

Thursday, Day 4 of 28

I drove up to Electronica's building determined to smash through all the closed doors. It started well when Emily greeted me in the lobby and handed me an access badge.

"You won't need me to get you into the building anymore," she said. She was wearing a perfume that smelled like a citrus grove by the ocean, and I momentarily forgot my new determination.

"Thank you, Emily," is all that I could come up with as I followed her up the stairs.

"You're welcome."

"Actually, I might need a little bit more of your help," I finally said regaining my wit.

"What can I do for you?"

We got to her desk, and I noticed pictures of her with a couple of teenage boys. However, there were no men in the pictures. She noticed me examining the photos and cleared her throat.

"Those boys look a bit old to be your sons," I said as a compliment and quickly realized that I might have been too indiscreet.

She smirked and said, "Those are my older sister's kids."

I was relieved to get out of that one. "Oh, that's great. So, I take it no family of your own yet?"

She shook her head no. "What was it that you wanted help with?"

So, I had a chance. Not married, no kids, and she smiled at me. I had to be careful not to screw this up. "Right. Sorry, I'm a bit distracted this morning."

She smiled at me again after I paused for a few seconds staring at her and proving again that I was distracted. I finally went on, "I was hoping that you could work your magic and get me an appointment with the VP of Engineering today."

Emily jumped on the computer and analyzed the schedule. "Sorry, it doesn't look good. The best I can do is tomorrow morning."

"No way you could squeeze me in today?" I said trying to be charming.

"Sorry. They kind of do their own thing over there."

Well, that confirmed my observation about the Engineering department. I was stuck and had to make the best of today.

"Ok, I understand. Thank you, Emily."

She smiled again, that is three times so far today, but then she turned away from me and went back to her work.

I walked over to my cube trying to work out my plan of action. I had to accomplish something today. I dropped off my backpack and walked over to the cube where Evan Kaminski was sitting. He was staring at his screen with hands hovering over the keyboard, the same way I saw him last time, as if he never left his desk.

"Would you mind joining me for a quick breakfast?" I said.

"Oh, hello," he jerked up startled to see me. "Sorry, I didn't see you there."

"Breakfast? My treat."

"Well..." he hesitated. "Actually, I didn't eat today yet, so yes, sure."

I sat across from Kaminski at a cafeteria table. He had his plate piled high with eggs, sausages, and bacon as if he only ate when somebody paid for it.

"Hungry?" I asked as I dug into my cup of boring oatmeal.

"Yes. Thank you."

"You're welcome. Happy to watch you eat the good stuff. Enjoy it while you can. My doctor said that I can't enjoy life anymore since I have high cholesterol."

He chuckled, but kept eating.

"So," I continued, "it looks like I have some free time today, so maybe you can tell me more about your quoting process."

He nodded his head but kept eating.

"I understand that you collect the cost assumptions from Purchasing and Operations, then you plug those numbers into your model, but maybe you can tell me about what happens next."

He chewed and swallowed. "It's pretty straight forward from there, I guess. I apply our productivity percentages on purchased parts…"

"You mean price reductions?" I interrupted.

"Yes, we assume the suppliers get more productive with time and are able to take cost out."

"And how do you know what percentage reductions to use?" I asked.

"Well, for example, the three percent annual productivity for purchased parts is based on what we require in our contracts with suppliers. Every year, contractually, they have to give us at least a three percent decrease on pricing."

I wrote in my notebook and said, "And why does Purchasing build that three percent into the contracts?"

"ISSUE #9: Productivity giveback distortion"

I could tell that he thought the answer was obvious, but took a few seconds before answering anyway. "Purchasing's objective is to get at least three percent in savings every year, so they build that into the contract. That's what our customers require of us also."

"So, you give your customers three percent every year also?"

"Sometimes even more, but we build in three percent annually into our customer contracts as well, so we add that into our business case."

"Meaning you increase the first-year price by twelve to fifteen percent so that you can give it back year after year?" I asked.

Kaminski looked at me as if he accidently told me a secret. "Yes," he replied cautiously.

"So, do you think your suppliers do the same?"

"Purchasing says they don't. They insist that suppliers work hard every year to improve their manufacturing process and supply chain to find savings."

"And what do you think?" I challenged him gently.

He thought about it for a few seconds, took a bite of his bacon, thought about it some more, then said, "I know we are not able to find three percent every year for our customers. We assume inflation of three percent in our business case on labor, electricity, and raw material prices because they keep going up and we can't change manufacturing processes or suppliers without a lengthy approval process with customers, so we have to build the annual givebacks into the first-year price. I suppose suppliers are probably doing the same thing to us."

I nodded, satisfied with his answer. "Interesting," I said. "So, you put the business case together, then Sales quotes the price to the customer. Now, what happens when the customer rejects the quote and you have to do a second round of quoting?"

"We do it over again, basically."

"How so?"

"Well, we go back to Engineering, Purchasing, Operations, Logistics, everyone that is involved with the cost assumptions, and we ask them to challenge all those assumptions."

"ISSUE #10: Everyone sandbagging the numbers"

I wrote in my notebook again. "You mean to sharpen their pencils?" I asked, remembering the phrase that the VP of Sales used in my first meeting at Electronica.

"Yes, exactly," he replied, happy that we were finally on the same page.

"And why don't they give you their best cost on the first iteration?"

His forehead furrowed like an accordion and the happiness was replaced with confusion again. "I don't know. I guess they know that the customer will ask for a lower price anyway so they hold something back just in case."

"And do you ever challenge their assumptions?"

"Yes, of course. That's basically my job. I have historical data and previous quotes, so I know what we should expect, but our products seem to always be different than before and I don't have any way to estimate what those changes should cost."

"Don't you use the cost estimators to help with that?" I asked.

He quickly shook his head. "No, we can't trust their numbers. Plus, they don't have the bandwidth to cost all the changes. They are mostly working on estimates for parts in production so that Purchasing has some ammunition when negotiating annual savings with suppliers."

"Do you ever visit your plants or supplier plants to develop your own estimates?"

He chuckled and almost choked on his sausage. "I wish I could. I'm stuck at my desk all day, every day. I've never been to any manufacturing plants."

Now I almost choked on my oatmeal. "You've never been to the plants?!" I shouted in whisper.

He shrugged, but did not say anything.

"Sorry," I said realizing that he might be offended. What seemed like an obvious thing to me might not be obvious to this young man. "Please don't be offended. I'm just surprised that you haven't had a chance to see the plants yet. This would be very helpful in your job."

I wrote in my notebook.

"ISSUE #11: Navigator has never seen the ship or the ocean"

"Do you have any other questions?" asked Kaminski. "I have to go back to my quotes, unfortunately."

"No, you've answered all my questions. Thank you."

* * *

I spent the rest of the afternoon analyzing the little material that I have been able to gather so far and began working on my presentation to the CEO, Bill Rasor, and his staff. All I needed was to get more information from Engineering, and I should have a good recommendation ready. If I had more time and a travel budget, I would also love to visit Electronica's manufacturing plant in North Carolina, but I had enough to go on. Then, I can be done with this wretched place and move on with my life.

I got back to my hotel room after grabbing a quick dinner at a local restaurant and laid down on the bed without undressing. After five days in this hotel room, its utilitarian design was now starting to resemble a prison cell. Nobody to talk to and nowhere to go. In the past, at least I could call my wife and listen to all her problems. Now, divorced, that was not an option either. All my friends were busy with their own lives and had no time to talk. I do not know why Jim thought this would be good for me. I never felt more alone in my life.

Friday, Day 5 of 28

I woke up the next day still wearing my clothes from the day before. Expecting another unpleasant day at Electronica, I decided to eat breakfast at the hotel and feed on some forced pleasantries from the hotel staff. After a quick shower, I got dressed and headed downstairs. A pleasant Latin American fellow named Omar welcomed me at the restaurant and seated me at a table by the window. A nice young waitress named Stephanie brought me some orange juice and coffee and, with a smile, showed me to the buffet. I soaked up the smiles and stored them in the back of my mind in preparation for the day ahead.

I scanned my new badge and got into the Electronica building. It was convenient, but I missed Emily waiting for me in the lobby. Perhaps, it was for the best that I did not get attached to her. Upon finishing my assignment, I would be gone and she would never see me again. It would be unfair for me to pretend like there is a future between us. Not that she had any feelings for me anyway. Let us be honest, I was just happy to protect my own feelings. Still, it would be nice to see her.

I said hello to Evan and Alex, dropped off my backpack in my cube, and headed straight for my appointment with the VP of Engineering, Tim Meadows. He was looking out of his corner office window when I arrived. He was a tall, fit man with a mostly bald head that projected intelligence and confidence. The sleeves of his designer white shirt were rolled up like he was ready to get some work done, but he was wearing a red tie that said that the work will be done by whoever sat across the table from him.

"Good morning," I said.

He turned around and smiled politely. "Good morning, Mr. Benson," he replied calmly, which confused me, because I was expecting his tone to be more aggressive. "Have a seat."

"Please call me Doug," I insisted.

"Sounds good. Feel free to call me Tim."

So far, so good. He seemed very casual and easy going. I was encouraged. "Thank you," I said as we sat at a small conference room table he had in his office.

"I apologize I could not meet with you earlier. There's a lot going on right now."

"No problem," I said trying to hide my disappointment at having to wait all week for this appointment. "I understand there's a quality issue that you and your team are dealing with right now."

He shifted in his chair as if the thought of it made him feel uncomfortable. "So, what is it that I can do for you, Doug?"

I noticed a slight change in his tone that made me feel like he was doing me a favor to talk to me. "Yes, let me get straight to the point," I said. "I didn't see you at the Monday meeting to discuss the Volta quote, but I assume you're familiar with it?"

"Of course," he said slightly annoyed.

"Perfect. I just want to learn more about the process you go through for the quotation, so…"

"Actually," he interrupted me, "let me stop you right there if you don't mind. My job and my team's job is not to quote business, but to design products that work."

He stared at me letting his words sink in. His gentle demeanor was confusing, because it sounded like he was saying pleasant things, but actually he was making a firm point that maybe was not so pleasant.

As I did not respond, he continued, "You see, Sales and Finance can run around trying to chase the numbers, but we actually have to get our designs to perform per customer requirements. And they have to perform not just on day one, but for many years to come and without breaking a single time. People's lives depend on our brake system to work every time."

He stared at me again as if I did not know what Electronica made and was unaware of how critical his job was.

"Understood," I said finally. "Outside of performance, though, what other requirements do you have to meet?"

"If you're referring to cost," he smiled, "then, yes, that is also one of the requirements. But cost doesn't matter when we can't meet customer requirements. I let Sales worry about getting the price we need from the customer. Plus, we have cost reduction activities after the product launches where we can take some cost out if needed."

I nodded and wrote in my notepad.

"ISSUE #12: No cost optimization during product development"

"Good," he said and stood up as if that concluded our meeting. "I'm glad you agree."

"Oh…" I replied a bit confused. "I do have more questions if you don't mind."

"Sure," he replied but did not sit back down. "What else would you like to know?"

"I guess one question that begs an answer is why not optimize cost during product development?" I asked naively.

He laughed then caught himself and got serious again. "Sorry, I didn't mean to laugh. I keep forgetting that you're not in automotive engineering."

I ignored the insult and let him go on.

"Optimizing for cost up front is nice in theory, but this is a low margin business. My resources have shrunk by twenty five percent in the last five years. My team is barely keeping up with the workload that we already have. At the same time, the customers want to go faster and faster to the market, so my product development times have shrunk from four or five years to three and sometimes two years. Oh, and don't forget, the products that the customers want are more and more complex. It's not just simple mechanical components anymore, now I have to spend half my budget on developing complex electronics and software that goes with it. I am squeezed between a rock and a hard place. Do you see?"

"Yes, I see," I responded somberly. "At the same time, though, and I apologize if I'm being too frank, Electronica has not won any business in two years. Don't you think that cost has to be considered at some point?"

"Cost is not my problem," he replied straining not to break his gentle tone with anger. "It's Purchasing's job to get our suppliers to lower their prices. Our cost estimators will tell you that we're paying at least ten percent too much already. And our plant's job is to control their cost. It's not Engineering's fault that they are running at fifty percent capacity."

He sat back in his leather chair and stared at me gently as I wrote in my notebook.

"ISSUE #13: Silo culture"

"Sorry," he continued, "I have another meeting to attend if you don't mind."

"Understood," I said trying not to sound annoyed at being cut off early in every meeting at Electronica so far. "I think I better understand your situation now. I appreciate your time."

He nodded and moved over to his computer screen. I took that as a good bye and left his office.

* * *

I spent the rest of the day working on a presentation for Bill Rasor. I had enough material now to make my recommendation, but held off on setting up a meeting with him just to make sure I had enough time over the weekend to finish it.

The issues that I wrote down during the interviews were guiding me in my recommendation. It was clear to me now what steps needed to be taken in order to fix this place. I kept looking over at the list as I built a framework.

ISSUE #1: Sharpening pencils to get to the numbers

ISSUE #2: Spread cost evenly on all products, like peanut butter on toast

ISSUE #3: Looking into the past instead of the future

ISSUE #4: Bad objectives drive wrong buyer behavior

ISSUE #5: Suppliers sandbagging the numbers

ISSUE #6: Supplier price estimates are point in time estimates only

ISSUE #7: Lack of supplier price validation

ISSUE #8: Misaligned objectives between functions

ISSUE #9: Productivity giveback distortion

ISSUE #10: Everyone sandbagging the numbers

ISSUE #11: Navigator has never seen the ship or the ocean

ISSUE #12: No cost optimization during product development

ISSUE #13: Silo culture

Monday, Day 8 of 28

I was in good spirits when I got up on Monday morning. After spending most of the weekend locked up in my room finalizing the presentation, I was ready to give a recommendation and be done with this project. I even booked my flight for the following day giving myself all day today for any follow up that Rasor or anyone on his staff might have.

I took my time getting ready and spent an hour reviewing the presentation at breakfast. My server, Stephanie, kept refilling my coffee every few minutes. She looked to be in her early 20s, with blonde hair, blue eyes, and a smile that lit up the room. Every time I ran into someone her age, I always thought that she could have been my daughter. It was a stupid thought, but I could not help myself. My wife and I tried to have kids when we first got married, and the closest we ever got was a miscarriage four months into my wife's only pregnancy. The baby was a girl who we never got to meet.

"You have a big presentation today?" she asked.

"Yes. It's a big one."

"And you're leaving us after that?" she asked, seemingly disappointed.

I thought her question was very sweet. Maybe constantly losing people in her life was sad for her. "Yes. I'm checking out tomorrow morning. Time to go home."

"Well, good luck to you. I'm sure you're gonna do great." She smiled and walked away.

What a great pick me up. I now felt even better about today. I went back to reviewing my presentation. The points were simple, but probably not what Rasor wanted to hear. I started with culture (see Figure 1.1), where it should all start in order to have a successful quoting process and ultimately profitable company.

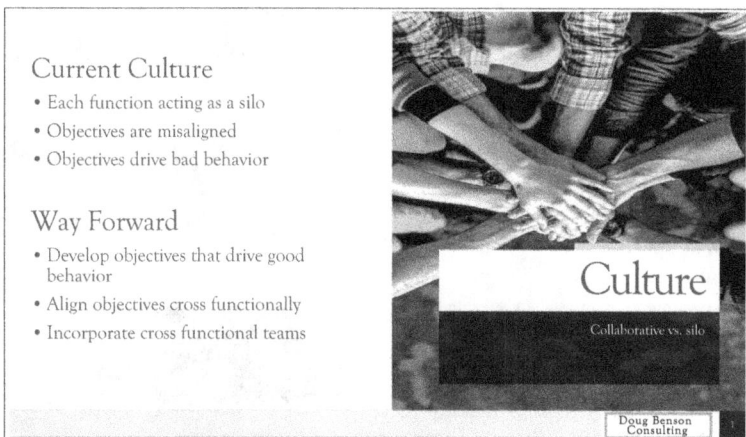

Figure 1.1 Culture presentation slide

It was very clear to me that Electronica's culture was not collaborative. Each function did its own thing and focused on their own objectives. Engineering was only focused on meeting product performance requirements, Purchasing was only focused on meeting annual savings objectives, Cost Estimating was only focused on cranking out estimates that were lower than supplier prices, Evan Kaminski was only focused on cranking out quotes, and Finance was only focused on reporting financial results. This separation of objectives into silos was driving a lot of bad behavior by individuals in each silo.

It was up to the upper management to fix this by setting objectives across all functions that were aligned. If the company wanted to grow profitably, then that objective should be on top of the list of everyone in the organization, from top to bottom. If everyone's pay was based on how much business they won and how profitable it was, they would align to help the quoting process and product development process to be successful. There was no point in existing as a business if the people working for the corporation were not aligned with its main objective.

The next most important facet of what needed to be addressed was people (see Figure 1.2). Closely aligned with culture, people acted the way the company's culture allowed them to act.

Figure 1.2 *People presentation slide*

Because of this, the people at Electronica did only what they were told and were not inspiring to do better. They stopped innovating and improving. They do not trust their management to help them step out of their boundaries.

What needed to happen was management had to release people to do what they were capable of doing. Every time I think of this effect, I think of young birds learning how to fly for the first time. I have been through this kind of transformation personally, and that is exactly how it made me feel. It sounds corny, but it is the truth, and it is that dramatic.

If culture and people can be taken care of, then they can be used as a foundation to build the rest. The product, which is the data and calculations, would be better and more accurate (see Figure 1.3).

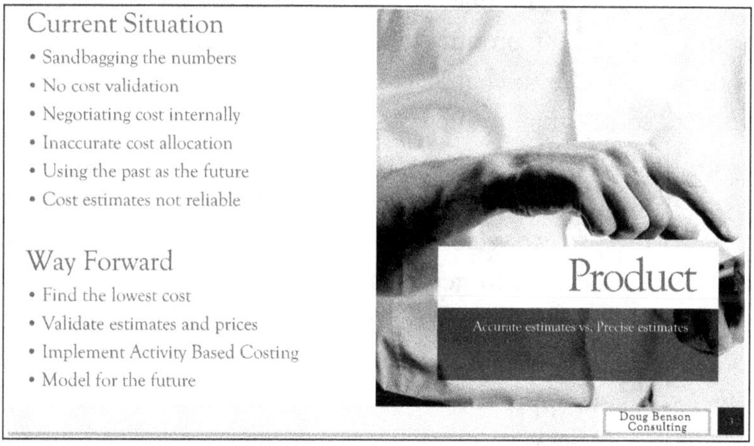

Figure 1.3 Product presentation slide

Instead of sandbagging the numbers to protect themselves and then negotiating internally to get to the highest cost possible for themselves, they would focus on seeking out the lowest possible cost that is feasible. Instead of hoping that the high cost will be good enough, they would challenge and validate costs using accurate cost estimating and allocating methods.

The process would also reflect the proper focus (see Figure 1.4). Currently, there is very little cost control throughout the

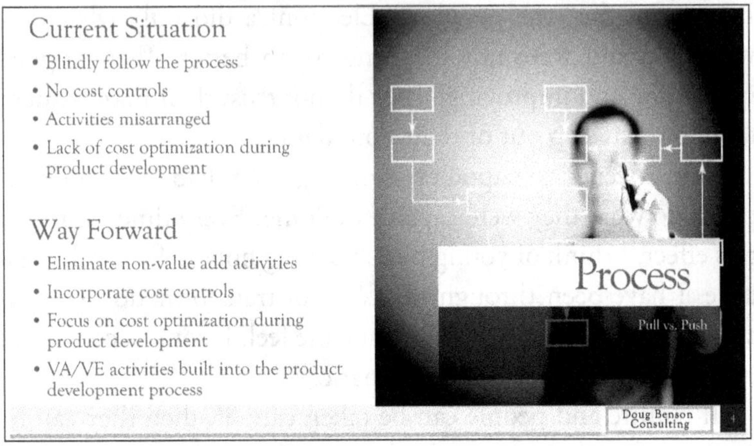

Figure 1.4 Process presentation slide

product development process. Purchasing, Operations, and Finance wait until Engineering finalizes the design, which could be months into the product development process, then, when it is already too late to change course, those functions go out and evaluate cost of the product.

With improved cost data, the process would be able to focus on early and frequent cost evaluation, even during the concept stage. If the project veers off course on cost, cost optimization tools would be used to get it back on track. Due to shortened development timing and lesser resources, all processes will have to be reworked to eliminate any wasted steps or unnecessary paperwork and approvals.

Finally, some very specific actions will have to be implemented (see Figure 1.5). A dedicated cross functional quoting team should be established, and instead of just collecting and reporting data, this team should be establishing cost targets for Electronica's manufacturing plants and suppliers. This would require close cooperation and detailed analysis as well as some smart forecasting of future optimal capacity utilization and probably many cost optimization strategies.

I closed my laptop and smiled with self-satisfaction. Rasor and his staff could not question my common-sense approach. The presentation pointed out some very obvious and self-evident

Detailed Recommendations

- Objective #1 across all functions should be growth in profitable business
- Dedicated cross functional team should be established for quoting
- Disciplined cost controls should be established during development and post production start
- Cost optimization should be built into the product development process
- Require VA/VE workshops between PD gates to drive innovation in achieving required functions
- Cost estimating should be employed in evaluating product designs
- Buyers should be engaged in negotiating with suppliers during quoting process
- Cost estimating should support supplier negotiations with cost data
- Saving achievement should be based on lifetime product cost, not one year only
- Built in productivity givebacks should be avoided in contracts if possible
- Cost assumptions should be based on future optimal state, not past accounting data
- Activity Based Costing should be utilized for proper cost allocation
- Quoting analyst should be developing cost assumptions and targets with the plants and suppliers
- Find the lowest cost achievable then negotiate with customers to get the highest price possible
- Assign continuous improvement projects to every manager

Figure 1.5 Detailed recommendations presentation slide

flaws. The solutions made sense. There was no way for them to challenge anything I have put together. Sure, I did not expect them to jump out of their seats with joy and raise me up on their shoulders in celebration, but they had to admit and accept the findings and the recommendations.

I finished my coffee and got up. Stephanie waved good bye with a smile, and I did the same. I nodded my head to Omar as I walked out of the restaurant.

"Have a great day, senior," he said.

"Yes, indeed, amigo," I replied with a bounce in my step.

* * *

I entered Electronica's lobby and rushed up the stairs. I dropped my stuff at the cubicle and was about to walk over to Emily's desk to set up an appointment with Rasor, when she appeared at my desk.

"Oh, good morning. I was about to come see you," I said surprised.

"Good morning. Bill would like to see you in his office," she replied dryly.

"Well, perfect," I exulted. "I was actually wanting to see him."

I grabbed my laptop and followed her to his office, which was a luxurious corner suite. I noticed a private bathroom and a small bedroom attached. As a CEO of a global company, I guess he must spend a lot of time here.

Rasor was sitting on a leather couch drinking what looked like a scotch on the rocks. "Please have a seat, Doug," he said and pointed at a large leather chair across from him. "Can I get you something to drink?"

"No, thank you." I sat down and opened my laptop to get ready for the presentation.

"No need for the laptop," he said calmly and took a sip of his drink.

"Oh, sorry. I assumed you wanted an update on my progress. I'm actually ready to give my recommendation."

"That won't be necessary, Doug."

"No problem. We can schedule for another time…"

"No," he interrupted, "I mean we won't need your recommendation."

"But, what…" I said trying to understand.

"We will not require your services. Your project has been canceled," Rasor said calmly and stared at me.

I was shocked and stared back at him without comprehending. His face did not reveal any feelings, and his calm in this situation made me uneasy. Was he enjoying letting me go or was he upset about it? I could not tell.

"Sorry, I'm confused," I said finally. "What has happened?"

Rasor put his drink on a coffee table between us and sat up straight. "There's not much to discuss. I appreciate your work, I'm sure your findings would have been interesting to see, but we've got too much going on right now." He stood up and extended his hand for a handshake. "Thank you, Doug. It was nice meeting you."

I was a bit dizzy from what just happened, but I stood up and shook his hand without saying a word.

"Have a good one," he said and walked over to his giant mahogany desk.

I stumbled out of his office and marched back to my cubicle.

CHAPTER 2

The Recovery

I was still dizzy from shock driving back to my hotel. I was already halfway there and now realized that I could not remember leaving Electronica or getting into my car or driving for that matter. I stopped at a red light and dialed my phone. The car's Bluetooth picked up the signal, and the phone's ringing filled the whole car.

"Hey, buddy!" boomed Jim Miller's voice when he finally picked up.

"I just got fired, Jim," I said flatly.

"Come again?"

"Your CEO, Bill Rasor, just fired me," I repeated with a bit of aggravation.

There was a moment of silence, then Jim let out a long sigh and said, "I'm sorry, Doug. I didn't know anything about it. They must have gone around me somehow." I did not respond and started to drive again when the light turned green.

"Did anything happen?" Jim continued after a short moment.

"Nothing happened. I spent the whole weekend working on the damn recommendation and was ready to present it to Rasor when he called me into his office and just fired me."

"Nothing happened before that? Did you piss anybody off?"

"Like who?" I said.

"I don't know. How about last week?" he pressed me.

"I didn't talk to Rasor at all before today. I just met with a bunch of people last week. They were all annoyed, especially your VP of Engineering, but no major arguments or anything."

"Wait!" Jim interrupted. "You spoke with Tim Meadows?"

"Yes. Why?"

"He actually let you meet with him? In his office?"

"Was he not supposed to?" I said, confused.

"Never mind. I think I know what happened."

"That's great, Jim, but honestly I don't really care. I'm flying home tomorrow."

"Wait, give me some time to figure this out," he pleaded.

"Why? Wait for what? I'm done with this place." My senses were coming back to me, and I was now getting angry.

"Doug, give me some time to figure this out. I'll call you back soon."

"I'm getting on that plane tomorrow," I said and hung up.

Tuesday, Day 9 of 28

I slept like a rock that night and felt refreshed when I woke up around 7:00 AM. The anger subsided, and I now felt as if a huge burden was taken off my shoulders. I was done with Electronica, and that felt good. My flight was at 11:00 AM, so I took my time packing my suitcase, then went downstairs for a relaxing breakfast. Omar and Stephanie greeted me with smiles as always.

"Excited to go home?" asked Stephanie.

"Yes, thank you." I said and smiled back.

She poured me some coffee as I sat down. I was looking forward to going home, but I would miss Stephanie and her smiley face every day for breakfast. Even when I was married, my wife was never a smiley type, and it got worse after the miscarriage. She was into her work, and I was into mine. Toward the end of our marriage, we barely even saw each other. We spent most of the evenings reading books or watching TV separately. Maybe we were just too sad to rekindle our love. It got away from us after 20 years of marriage.

My phone rang suddenly and startled me out of my melancholy.

"Good morning, Jim," I said with sarcastic enthusiasm as I picked up the phone.

"Good. I'm glad you picked up. I have some good news." He sounded winded, and I heard some noises in the background.

"Me too. I slept great, I feel great, and my plane leaves in three hours."

"You're not going anywhere, Doug!" Jim exclaimed.

"Oh, yes I am," I contradicted him.

"I spoke with the board last night. Tim Meadows pulled the strings to get you fired, but they are all back online now."

"I didn't know that Meadows runs Electronica. I thought that Rasor was the CEO."

"Meadows is buddies with one of the directors, Robert Sterling, who used to be the CEO of Electronica. They are both engineers and into fishing, so that's what happened."

"You know what?" I said remembering that it really did not matter to me anymore. "I really don't care. You can deal with that yourself."

There was a pause on the phone for a moment. Stephanie dropped off an egg white omelet at my table, and I took a bite.

"I would like to offer you a Vice President position at Electronica," Jim finally said.

I almost choked on my omelet. "What? You want me to stay here permanently?" I shouted and then laughed. Other restaurant guests and staff turned to look at me. I raised my hand in apology and whispered into the phone, "Jim, there is no way in hell that I'm going back to that place."

"It will only be until you can implement all your recommendations and find a successor. Of course, we'd have to win that Volta business first."

"And what if our cost structure doesn't support the price and we don't win the business?" I asked.

"You would stay on until it is competitive, of course."

I was always a sucker for a challenge, and I was suddenly having a hard time resisting the temptation to take on turning Electronica around. As exciting as it was to go home again, I was getting goosebumps thinking about all the fun I would be having fixing Electronica and winning that Volta business.

"Why can't you do this yourself?" I finally asked him.

"I'm at the airport right now and will be landing there in three hours."

"Oh, so what do you need me for?"

"Don't play dumb, Doug. You're the best cost engineering guy in the country, maybe the world. I will be there to support you and get people lined up, but I need you to fix it."

I felt a bit ashamed for drawing some praise out of him, but it did feel good to hear it. Between Electronica and my divorce, I have not heard too many positive things said about me, and I needed a boost of self-confidence.

"I want the title of Cost Engineering VP with Evan Kaminski, that Kumar guy, and those teams reporting to me," I demanded.

"You got it, Doug," he replied quickly.

"And I want a dedicated cross-functional quoting team and process under me."

"Done."

Stephanie stopped by and started to refill my coffee.

"Anything else?" asked Jim.

"I want a suite at my hotel," I said finally and smiled at Stephanie.

"You got it," he replied. "I'll see you at Electronica at one o'clock."

I heard a click as he hung up. I looked up at Stephanie who was still standing there next to my table.

"Extending your stay with us?" she asked.

"Yes, I'm afraid you'll be stuck with me for a while longer."

* * *

I have to admit, I was looking forward to the fireworks as I drove up to Electronica's office that afternoon. Jim was already there, and I assumed he was already clearing a way for me, but I wanted to see the look on everyone's faces as I walked in exonerated.

"Good morning, Doug," said Emily, as she welcomed me in the lobby. She seemed genuinely happy to see me, which took me aback.

"Well, good morning, Emily."

"I have a new badge for you and I want to take you to your new office."

I felt like I was just given the VIP access to an exclusive night club as she walked me up to a spacious office with a great view of the city. It literally made me feel like I was on top of the world.

"Thank you, Emily. This is perfect."

"You have a two o'clock with Jim, Bill, and the executive team to present your recommendations. We don't have an admin assigned to you yet, so I'll be taking care of you in the meantime. Please let me know if you need anything."

I smiled happily with the thought of having Emily around. She took that as a confirmation and left my office.

* * *

Feeling good about myself did not last long. As soon as I walked into the executive conference room and faced all the same designer suits as my first meeting at Electronica, my stomach dropped and all my confidence left me. It did not even help that Rasor greeted me with a smile and sat me next to him at the big conference table or that my friend, Jim, the full six-feet and four inches of him, was there to support me. I could not get out of my mind the fact that most of these executives wanted me out of here just a day ago.

"Team!" shouted Rasor over the murmur in the room. "I would like you to give a round of applause to Doug Benson for becoming our VP of Cost Engineering."

The room erupted in a halfhearted round of clapping. I smiled and raised my hand in halfhearted thank you.

"Welcome to the team, Doug," said Jim after the clapping stopped. "We are looking forward to hearing your recommendations."

I spent the next hour going through my presentation describing each point in detail, from the cultural elements to the process, the people, and the product, which was the data that needed to be produced. Everyone in the room behaved professionally, but I could tell from some of the body language that my observations and recommendations made some people uncomfortable.

The VP of Engineering, Tim Meadows, seemed aloof and kept looking at his watch, clearly not buying into what I was saying.

Considering he was the reason for my firing a day ago, I knew that he only listened to my presentation because Jim was in the room. Others, like the VP of Finance, George Sewell, and Ricardo Rodriguez, the VP of Purchasing, whom I have not talked to before, seemed not too pleased with my presentation. It was like watching someone try to eat snails or crickets for the first time. Only the VP of Sales, Pete Jones, and the VP of Operations, Bud Kulig, seemed genuinely interested in what I was saying. Perhaps, they were the only ones truly seeking a change in order to win business and fill the plants, respectively.

"Excellent!" exclaimed Jim after I was done. His wavy blond hair shook energetically as he spoke and his recently purchased white teeth beamed with confidence. "This is exactly what I was looking for."

I was not sure how Jim and I became friends in college. He came from money, which he never talked about, and I came from a low middle-class family, which I complained about all the time, but somehow we clicked right away. It was probably more to his credit that the relationship worked, he was so positive and easy going that it negated any of my skepticism and sarcasm. "Thank you, Jim. Are there any questions from the team?" I asked.

Rasor stood up and walked to the back of his chair. "Having said all that, what do you want from this team, Doug? You'll have your team to work with, but what do you need from us?"

"Exactly what you just said is what we need to address," I replied. "It's not just my team that will be solely responsible for our success. Cost engineering is a cross-functional team sport. We will need everyone in this room to be aligned."

"You can count on it, Doug," exclaimed Rasor nodding toward Jim with reassurance.

"I appreciate it, Bill, but we need more than words and good intentions," I said quickly and watched Rasor defensively puff out his chest like a rooster, so I quickly added, "No offense, Bill, but I believe this collaboration needs to be institutionalized. It needs to be just the way we do business. Ultimately, it needs to be part of our culture or who we are."

"What do you have in mind specifically, Doug?" asked Jim.

"I propose that we first align everyone in this room to the same objective, which should be profitable growth. That should be worth at least fifty percent of everyone's performance objective, perhaps more, considering this is the primary reason companies exist."

"My number one goal is to design parts that work, are you suggesting I should not care about that anymore?" spoke up Tim Meadows.

"On the contrary, Tim," I replied calmly. "Designing parts that work is one of the requirements of growing profitably. But, it's only one of the requirements. Other requirements are for the parts to be manufacturable and cost effective, for example. And, what I'm saying is that everyone in this room must care about meeting every requirement, not just the one that is most important to any one function or person."

I looked around the room and was met with silence. Change is hard, and I expected these guys to resist it naturally. Executives and managers were chosen to do a job because they were thought to be good at delivering on specific objectives. By changing objectives, the reasons for them being there were automatically challenged, and their careers put in jeopardy. At least, that is how people often felt.

"This is one item that I need the team in this room to address," I continued. "The other way to institutionalize a cost engineering culture is to include it in the product development process. I'd like this team to consider adding mandatory cost checks and cost optimization activities directly in the process. This way, it's not something I alone am driving, but something that we are all required to do."

"My chief of program management will not be happy about this," spoke up Meadows again. "He can barely meet the program timing now."

"I agree," I said trying to sound sympathetic. "However, what is the point of meeting the program timing if the product launches at no profit?"

"Pete can make up for that by negotiating price increases on any changes that Volta makes, right Pete?" said Meadows smiling at the VP of Sales.

"You got it," said Jones and smiled back at Meadows.

"That's great," I agreed. "We'll need all the profit we can get, because we'll have to give it back to the customer after year one anyway. And, we'll do that every year until the end of program at about a three percent clip."

Everyone's faces darkened, and the smiles disappeared. I continued, "In my estimation, in order for us to meet our customer's pricing demands, we must significantly reduce our cost structure, including our material cost. This is the only way we can win the Volta business or any business after that."

A murmur went around the room, so Jim stood up and said, "Doug is right. We must make drastic changes to turn things around. Leave it to me and this team, Doug, to address your recommendations. I'm sure everyone in this room is committed to making this company successful. We'll meet separately to figure out how to address your points."

"Thank you, Jim," I said.

"Anything else you need from us?" threw in Rasor, and I could not tell if he was being sarcastic.

"I'll be working with all of you to implement the rest. I just ask for full cooperation," I said as I looked around the room. "We don't have a lot of time to turn this around."

"Perfect!" exclaimed Jim.

And, so it started.

Wednesday, Day 10 of 28

As I woke up the next day, it dawned on me that the real work has just began. The recommendation part, as difficult as it seemed before, was the easy part. I suddenly became panicked about my ability to pull off the turnaround. What if we make all the changes to the process and still lose the Volta business? Fair or unfair, Rasor and his staff could easily call that a failure of my efforts and philosophy. I decided to skip breakfast and rush straight to the office.

I had a meeting arranged the day before, so my new team was waiting for me in a conference room at 8:00 AM sharp. Evan, Alex, Kumar, and his two cost estimators were all arranged around a conference room table quietly staring at each other, not sure what to say or what the meeting was even about.

"Good morning, team," I announced as I walked into the room. "Are you ready to rock and roll?" That sounded too phony in my own mind, but these guys needed an injection of some energy. Their feeble nods told me that I failed so far. "In case you're wondering why you're here," I continued, "we've reorganized and you all work for me now. I am the new VP of Cost Engineering and you are now part of the new Cost Engineering group."

They all looked confused, and Evan quickly raised his hand. "I have a question," he said.

"Go ahead. And, you don't have to raise your hand to ask questions."

"What is cost engineering and what are our jobs now?"

I smiled and said, "Right. Great question. I guess I never really explained to you guys the basic concept of cost engineering. To put it simply, cost engineering is designing and developing parts to meet pre-defined cost requirements or targets. So, instead of designing parts and then worrying about the cost later, we want to define the cost first, then work to design parts while we pay attention to the required cost throughout the product development process."

"So, am I not quoting anymore?" said Evan.

"Well, yes, but you can stop all your activities for now. All your quotes will go to waste anyway if we keep doing it wrong. We'll be focusing exclusively on the Volta business and starting from scratch at that."

"What about us, sir?" asked Kumar pointing at himself and his two associates.

"You also can stop all your current activities. Your team will be focusing exclusively on the Volta BOM."

"Sir, but we already estimated most of those parts," Kumar pointed out.

"And that's a great start. However, now you and your team will be supporting our negotiation with the suppliers."

Kumar almost fell out of his chair. "But, sir, we don't negotiate with suppliers, Purchasing does that."

"You do now," I insisted, "together with Purchasing. And, you don't have to call me 'sir.' Please call me Doug."

The room was quiet as they all tried to absorb the new information.

"In case you're wondering what's next," I continued, "we have a busy week next week. Evan, Alex, and I will be flying out Monday morning to visit our plant in North Carolina." I paused to observe the shock on Evan's and Alex's faces. "We need to see with our own eyes what's happening on the manufacturing floor and what that means in terms of cost. And, we'll be developing a cost model for that plant. Please spend the next couple of days preparing all of your Volta information, including anything that you have received from the plant."

Evan and Alex nodded their heads, still a bit dazed.

"In the meantime, Kumar," I went on, "I need you to please prepare all of your cost estimates for the housing, the machined aluminum block, and the header. You and your team will be meeting up with us starting on Wednesday in South Carolina at the supplier plants for those three components. The buyers will meet us there and we'll be negotiating pricing with the suppliers."

Kumar's face was now agape, and his two associates were tightly gripping their chair arms as if expecting an earthquake. However, none of them said anything.

"Great!" I expounded. "Are there any questions?"

They all shook their heads.

"Perfect! In that case, welcome to the team and let's win that Volta business. This company is counting on us to get it done and I'm confident that you have the right talent and skill to do just that."

They looked at me like I was some kind of a wild preacher. I knew that they probably have not heard anyone speak like that to them at Electronica, but I also knew that we needed everyone motivated to succeed. I had to raise their spirits and get them excited about our mission.

* * *

My next challenge that day was engineering. I had a meeting set up with Meadows, and I expected a lot of resistance from him. He was waiting for me in his office, and his arms were already crossed defensively before I even started talking.

"Thank you for taking the time to meet with me, Tim," I began. He only nodded and gave a little smirk, so I continued. "I will get straight to it. We have a twenty-four-dollar problem on the Volta business." I put a piece of paper in front of him with a breakdown (see Table 2.1).

Table 2.1 Target cost breakdown

	Target	Current	Gap
Price	$100.00	$121.32	$21.32
Profit	$10.00	$7.29	($2.71)
Cost	$90.00	$114.03	$24.03

Meadows looked at the numbers for few seconds and said, "That's a sandbagging problem that you need to resolve with our plant and Purchasing. We gave the best design that we could come up with, there's nothing else Engineering can do to help you."

"I disagree," I said assertively. "I agree that sandbagging is a problem, but it's only half the problem. The other half is the design and we'll never get to the target price if we don't address it."

Meadows took in a long breath in frustration as if though he was about to blow fire at me, so I continued, "And I know that you think that Sales needs to convince Volta to pay more for our superior design, but the truth is that Volta's buyer can only do so much. If they have a quote from another supplier at $100 or somewhere around that, then he won't be able to convince his executive management that they should pay $20 or even $10 more for our design."

"What do you suggest we do, then, start from scratch?" finally said Meadows. "We don't have time or resources."

"I'm attacking this thing from all angles. I will be working with both the plant and suppliers next week onsite and I need your team in a one-day cost reduction workshop this Friday."

"This Friday?" shouted Meadows, and even he was surprised by his uncharacteristic response.

"Yes, this Friday. I will lead the workshop but I need your whole Volta team to participate."

"I can't afford to spare my team for a whole day," he resisted.

"I'll be frank, Tim," I interrupted, "you can't afford not to. If we don't win this Volta business, your resources will be cut and you might not have a team at all."

"Is that a threat?" he suddenly stiffened.

"That's the reality and Jim will tell you the same thing. There won't be anything to design if we don't win this Volta business. There won't be much for anyone to do, period."

Meadows stared at me, but did not say a word. I was trying to be honest, but I think he was still taking my words purely as a threat. I did not mean for it to sound that way, but perhaps that was the only way to get through to this guy.

"I will send a meeting invite for this Friday," I said. "Please have your team bring in the drawings and any competitor parts to benchmark if you have them. I will do the rest."

He said nothing, so I nodded as though we had an agreement and walked out of his office. I guess we will have to find out on Friday if he will play along or not.

* * *

My next appointment was with Ricardo Rodriguez, the VP of Purchasing. I have not met with him before, so I did not know what to expect. All I knew was that he was originally from Spain and had a disposition of a bull fighter. However, considering that I would be asking him to completely change his modus operandi, I expected some resistance.

I found him in his office on the opposite side of the building from my office and also with a nice window view. I heard him yelling at someone as I approached.

"I don't give a shit about your situation, I want one million this year or you're never getting any business from me!" he screamed with a slight Spanish accent into his cell phone as I peeked into the office. He saw me standing at his door, but completely ignored me. "I don't care," he continued, "when I see you here on Tuesday, you better have a check in your hand or I'll have the security guard walk you out." Despite the display of anger, his well-groomed body and long hair showed no emotion or distress. It was as if yelling was his normal state of being. "Bye," he said to the phone and hung it up.

"Is it a good time to talk?" I asked him while still standing at the doorway.

"Yes, of course," he replied as if nothing extraordinary has happened. "Have a seat."

I obeyed and sat at a chair on the other side of his desk. "Thank you for taking the time to meet with me," I said.

"It's not like I had a choice. Your friend, Jim, made me do it," he replied bluntly.

"Well, it's for a good cause, so I'm sure you won't mind." That sounded lame, but he did catch me off guard with his frankness.

"What do you need?" he said sharply.

"Ok, let's jump right into it," I replied, again caught off guard. This guy obviously liked to shock people. "I need meetings set up next week with three of your suppliers in their South Carolina plants and I need your buyers there to help with the negotiation."

"Help?" he asked, puzzled. "My buyers are the only ones responsible for supplier negotiations."

"This will be a data-driven negotiation, digging deep into the cost, and it will have to be a team effort."

He stared at me for a moment, then said, "You can meet with one supplier and it will be here, in our corporate office. I don't have resources to spare for more, I need my team one hundred percent focused on this year's savings."

So, he wanted to negotiate. Always negotiate seemed to be the motto of all purchasing people I have ever met.

"I'm afraid my request is non-negotiable, Ricardo. In fact, there is more. I will also need those three suppliers to provide detailed cost breakdowns for their components by this Friday."

This time he was caught off guard. "That's impossible," he finally busted out, "I have negotiations to get ready for next week."

"Since you've been frank with me, Ricardo, I will be frank with you. I know that you're not focused on future programs, but you won't have much of a negotiation for this year's savings if we don't win some business. Your suppliers are not stupid, they see your volumes going down. Do you think they're spending time worrying about you or are they spending time banging on the doors of your competition who's taking your business away?"

He did not respond, so I continued, "Again, thank you for your time, I appreciate your support on this and I look forward to working with you and your buyers to win some business for us to leverage." He just stared at me calmly. His eyes seemed to say that he might be plotting an assassination attempt on me, which gave me a chill, but I took his silence for agreement and walked out of his office.

Thursday, Day 11 of 28

Days were flying by, and there were only a couple of weeks left until the Volta quote was due. Those remaining two weeks will be very busy, but today, I only had a meeting with Jim, so I took my time getting ready in the morning. Omar greeted me as always at the hotel restaurant and Stephanie quickly brought me my standard orange juice and coffee.

"Great to have you staying with us for a bit longer," she said with her usual bright smile.

"Yes, thank you, it might be a while before you get rid of me," I replied and returned her smile. "Electronica gave me a full-time job, so I'll be living here until I find my own place or until they fire me."

"That's great news! I guess I'll be seeing you a lot then," she said with genuine excitement.

"Don't get too excited, most people can only take so much of me, so you may get tired of me soon."

She laughed. "You're silly," she said as she waved her arm at me dismissively. "Well, help yourself to the buffet. Let me know if you need anything, I'll be in the kitchen for a little bit. I'm studying for a big test tonight. Just don't tell anyone, please."

"Oh, no problem at all. What are you studying?"

"Marketing, actually," she said shyly as if it was embarrassing to study anything. "I'm hoping to get a job in website design or sales or something like that."

"That's great. I wish you all the best on your test. I'm sure you'll do great," I assured her even though I had no idea if she would be capable of any such thing. Maybe it was just her positive energy that made me feel confident in her abilities.

"Thank you. That's very nice of you," she said.

"Please call me Doug," I threw out, feeling good about having someone to talk to. I guess she was becoming part of my little hotel family.

"Thank you, Doug. I will," she confirmed and went into the kitchen.

What a nice kid, I thought. It seems like every time I talked to her, I felt better about my day and my life in general. I had no idea how she managed to make me feel that way, but I was glad to have her there every morning to get my day started.

* * *

Jim was waiting for me alone in a conference room. He was standing by a white board looking at what looked like an org chart. There were boxes under each name filled with what looked like objectives.

"So I take it you wanted to see me about defining objectives?" I asked him.

"Just want to get your opinion. I drew something up based on your general recommendation, but I thought I'd run the details by you before we have HR launch this officially."

"Sure. Let's do it," I said enthusiastically, happy to see that Jim took my recommendation to heart.

Jim went on summarizing his thoughts, and I put it together in a matrix as he kept explaining (see Table 2.2). Each VP and his team would now have objectives boiled down to maximum five items, and everyone in their departments would have the same objectives and weights. Also, every department would share one objective in common, which would be to achieve profitable growth of 10 percent annually.

"What do you think?" asked Jim.

I stared at the matrix for a while, then said, "I like that you have the profitable growth as an objective for everyone, but I think we need to be bold and give it more weight across all functions. Do you mind if I make some changes?" I saw him nod in agreement, so I started crossing things out in the matrix. After I was done, we stood and looked at the modified matrix for a while (see Table 2.3).

"Let me explain," I said, seeing that Jim was not sold. "First, the only thing that matters to you and the shareholders is that you are profitable and the company grows, so that should be the biggest chunk of the objectives, at least 50% for each function. For my department, it's 65% because that's really the only reason we exist. Second, I decreased weights on some other objectives because they are less important or are already part of the profitable growth objective."

"But don't you want engineering developing new products?" he asked.

"They will have to if they want to grow and be profitable. The first objective alone will drive the behavior of innovation."

He nodded and said, "All right, how about purchasing, though? I mean their primary objective now is to find annual savings and you eliminated that completely."

"Great question, Jim. And that's exactly what is driving your BOM costs to be too high. Because suppliers need to find savings for you every year, they are forced to increase their prices so that they can meet those requirements. And guess what? Your

Table 2.2 Jim Miller proposal for companywide objectives

	CEO	Weight	VP of Engineering	Weight	VP of Purchasing	Weight
1	Profitable growth of 10% annually	50%	Profitable growth of 10% annually	25%	Profitable growth of 10% annually	25%
2	Return on investment of 20% annually	20%	Successful launch of new programs	35%	Successful launch of new programs	35%
3	Stock price growth of 10% annually	20%	Development of new products	30%	Achievement of 5% in annual savings	30%
4	Maintenance of positive corporate culture	5%	Maintenance of positive corporate culture	5%	Maintenance of positive corporate culture	5%
5	Maintenance of positive corporate citizenship	5%	Maintenance of positive customer relationships	5%	Maintenance of positive supplier relationships	5%
		100%		100%		100%

	VP of Operations	Weight	VP of Finance	Weight	VP of Cost Engineering	Weight
1	Profitable growth of 10% annually	25%	Profitable growth of 10% annually	50%	Profitable growth of 10% annually	50%
2	Return on investment of 20% annually	35%	Return on investment of 20% annually	20%	Return on investment of 20% annually	20%
3	Achievement of 5% in annual savings	30%	Accurate financial reporting	20%	Accurate cost estimating	20%
4	Maintenance of positive corporate culture	5%	Maintenance of positive corporate culture	5%	Maintenance of positive corporate culture	5%
5	Maintenance of positive corporate citizenship	5%	Maintenance of positive corporate citizenship	5%	Maintenance of positive supplier relationships	5%
		100%		100%		100%

Table 2.3 Doug Benson revised objectives matrix

	CEO	Weight	VP of Engineering	Weight	VP of Purchasing	Weight
1	Growth Profitable growth of 10% annually at 10% profit	50% 25%	Growth Profitable growth of 10% annually at 10% profit	50% 25%	Growth Profitable growth of 10% annually at 10% profit	50% 25%
2	Return on investment of 20% annually	20%	Successful launch of new programs	35%	Successful launch of new programs	35%
3	Stock price growth of 10% annually	20%	Development of new products	20%	Improvement in sourcing processing of 10% annually Achievement of 5% in annual savings	5% 30%
4	Maintenance of positive corporate culture	5%	Maintenance of positive corporate culture	5%	Maintenance of positive corporate culture	5%
5	Maintenance of positive corporate citizenship	5%	Maintenance of positive customer relationships	5%	Maintenance of positive supplier relationships	5%
		100%		100%		100%

	VP of Operations	Weight	VP of Finance	Weight	VP of Cost Engineering	Weight
1	Growth Profitable growth of 10% annually at 10% profit	50% 25%	Growth Profitable growth of 10% annually at 10% profit	50% 25%	Growth Profitable growth of 10% annually at 10% profit	65% 50%
2	Return on investment of 20% annually	35%	Return on investment of 20% annually	20%	Return on investment of 20% annually	20%
3	Optimization of mfg. processes Achievement of 5% in annual savings annually	5% 30%	Accurate financial reporting	20%	Accurate cost estimating	5% 20%
4	Maintenance of positive corporate culture	5%	Maintenance of positive corporate culture	5%	Maintenance of positive corporate culture	5%
5	Maintenance of positive corporate citizenship	5%	Maintenance of positive corporate citizenship	5%	Maintenance of positive supplier relationships	5%
		100%		100%		100%

purchasing team has no choice but to pretend like that is not happening because otherwise they would never be able to meet your annual savings requirements."

"But isn't that a standard practice in the automotive industry?" he interrupted.

"That doesn't make it right or smart," I retorted. "What your purchasing team should be focusing on solely is sourcing at the lowest price possible and the lowest lifetime cost possible, which they will if fifty percent of their objectives is profitable growth."

Jim scratched his head. "I don't even know if this is a skill set that we can easily shift to. For years, we've been trying to hire buyers that are good at getting us annual savings. And Ricardo is the best of them. I'm afraid he would quit if I turned his world upside down."

"Are you hiring to fit personal skills or are you hiring to meet company's objectives?"

He looked at me like I was trying to be a smart ass. "Do you always have to make sense, Doug?"

"That's what you pay me for," I said smiling.

"I'm sure you also have a good explanation for changing the objectives for the VP of Operations, but I'd like to hear why it's a bad thing for him to find five percent of savings every year."

"He'll do that now anyway because the bulk of his objectives is to grow profitably. On the other hand, having his objective to only find annual savings actually drives a bad behavior. Since costs keep going up due to inflation, it is almost impossible to reduce cost for a factory, so the natural instinct is to hold some back up-front. That way, the cost reductions are easier to achieve later in production."

"You're telling me that they are lying to us about their cost at the quote level?" he said somewhat taken back.

"You left them no choice," I stated frankly.

"Dang it. You're probably right again," he said in frustration but also in jest.

"So it's settled?" I asked. "It would really help our cause if you went with this."

Jim smiled and said, "I love it and you got a deal, buddy."

* * *

I stayed late at the office that day getting ready for the work-shop with Engineering. My desk was now buried in various papers, and I looked more and more like Evan Kaminski staring into my computer screen with fingers ready to pounce on my keyboard. I did not even notice when Emily stopped by my cubicle.

"Working late?" she asked, startling me.

"Yes, sorry, I didn't see you there."

"No, I'm sorry. I didn't mean to startle you."

I could not tell if she was being sincere or sarcastic. It felt like she might have been making fun of me for the ease with which I was startled.

"Other than making fun of me, is there another reason for why you stopped by?" I tried a little humor hoping to charm her a little.

She chuckled, then said, "Just wanted to let you know that I won't be your admin anymore. Helping Bill, Jim and you is just too much, so Jim asked that you hire your own admin."

It was very difficult to tell if she liked me. I was getting this hot and cold thing every time I talked to her. On the one hand, she laughed at my joke, and on the other, she was quitting as my admin. I decided to settle this once and for all.

"Oh, that's perfect actually," I said.

Her brow folded in confusion. "Why is that?" she replied and gave me hope because she almost sounded upset with my comment.

"Well, since you don't work for me anymore, I would like to ask you out to dinner this weekend."

She paused and stared at me blankly.

"I'm flexible on day and time," I continued. "And you can pick whichever restaurant you like most. I actually don't know what's good around here."

She continued to stare at me for a few more seconds that seemed like an eternity to me. "Saturday at six PM at 'The Ducky's.' I'll meet you there," she said finally and walked away.

I was in shock because I expected a complete rejection. I stared back at the screen again, then pumped my fists in the air. I was in the game.

Friday, Day 12 of 28

The day of the engineering workshop was finally here. I skipped breakfast and arrived at the office early around 6 AM. I reserved the biggest conference room in the building with about 20 chairs and several tables. As I requested from Engineering, torn down parts, both ours and competitors', were spread out on one of the tables in the corner of the room.

My team arrived at 7 AM. They seemed excited and suspicious at the same time. They had several large printouts with them, and I had them hang those up on the wall. Among them were the Volta part drawings, cost breakdowns, and manufacturing plant layout.

"Do you think Engineering or Purchasing will show up?" asked Evan.

"They will," I assured him.

Sure enough, people from Engineering and Purchasing started to roll in slowly prior to the 8 AM start time. They all seemed pretty sleepy and somewhat disinterested. It was obvious they were here only because they had to. Most got on their laptops as soon as they arrived. Fortunately, Emily had ordered some breakfast sandwiches and doughnuts with good coffee, which picked up the mood in the room.

By 8:05 AM, we had a full room, including Tim Meadows and Ricardo Rodriguez whom I asked to join us. We were ready to start.

"Good morning everyone," I shouted to quiet down the conversations in the room. I got a weak "good morning" back from the participants, half of them still staring at their laptops. "Thank you all for joining us today. Before I get into the details, first rule of the workshop is that there will be no laptops on. So, please put them down now."

A murmur of dissatisfaction went through the room. This was always the most unpopular part of any workshop I have ever done, but it was best to set the rules now rather than try to implement them later. Fortunately, everyone followed my request.

"Thank you," I continued. "The reason for no laptops is that I will need your undivided attention all day. These type of VA/VE workshops take normally three to five days at a minimum and we only have one day and a lot of material to squeeze into that one day. Also, don't expect this to be a lecture by me. I'm not planning to stand here to talk all day. You will be actively participating in the exercises and you will be leading this effort."

I looked around the room and saw a lot of eyes glazed over, still not comprehending their role in the workshop. "You are probably asking why we are doing it and why you are here," I went on. "You deserve the truth so I'll be frank with you. It's because this company is in a critical situation and we need all hands on deck. You've all been hired to do a specific job and you can probably find another job somewhere else, but this company needs you. If we don't win this Volta program, you or your colleagues might have to find new jobs. And believe me, it won't be fun or pleasant watching Electronica go into a death spiral. There won't be anything cool to design and there won't be any supplier negotiations if this company loses the Volta program."

I watched as everyone shifted uncomfortably in their chairs. Meadows and Rodriguez stared at me as if I was high on drugs. I was quite sure they never spoke to their teams in this frank manner, and I expected it to be a bit of a shock, but they needed an adrenaline shot to have a chance of being successful in this workshop and in winning the Volta business. "Tim and Ricardo are here today to kick off the workshop because they wanted you guys to know that it is important to them as well. They are counting on you. And, they will come in later today to see you report on the workshop results."

One of the engineers, Josh Donaldson, a skinny young man with glasses that did not fit properly, raised his hand and spoke up without waiting for my permission. "What is actually the problem that we're planning to solve here? Because my design on the Volta program is pretty damn good, I don't know what else can make it better."

"Great question, Josh. Perfect segue into my next point. What is the problem that we're trying to solve here? As you know, this is a cost reduction workshop, so what we'll be trying to improve is cost. Why? Because we have a twenty-four-dollar problem. In order to guarantee that we win the Volta business, we need to take out twenty-four-dollars from the current cost."

The room erupted in frustration. Some folded their arms and shook their heads, some laughed, and one of the engineers even opened his laptop as if to give up on the effort completely.

"That's impossible," exclaimed Donaldson. "That's twenty percent of the price that we quoted."

I let them stew for a few moments. "Yes, I agree," I finally said. "The mountain we have to climb is daunting. This is why we are having this emergency workshop and all of you here. This is not going to be a walk in the park. We'll have to use our collective brain power to figure this out. Right now you're looking up at the mountain and you're ready to give up because it looks high and steep and it seems impossible to get to the top. But, I want you to think of it as climbers do, one step at a time. Climbers climb the mountain section by section, not in one leap. We'll have to do the same. We'll have to chip away at the mountain, one step at a time, one idea at a time. And this workshop is just the beginning of our journey. After we come up with ideas here, and we will come up with ideas, then we'll have to implement those ideas. That's the hard part. This workshop is actually going to be the easy and fun part. It's out of your comfort zone, but you'll be surprised to discover at the end that this exercise was actually pretty fun. We'll be opening our minds and being creative. That's fun. You won't be staring at your screen today, you will be using your brain and creativity. That's fun."

I looked around the room again. I could not tell if my motivational speech was having an effect. I continued only after some arms have unfolded and that one laptop closed again. "Great! Let's get started then."

I thanked Meadows and Rodriguez for being with us and told them to come back at 4 PM for a report out. They seemed skeptical, but tried to hide it. Regardless, they promised to be back.

"All right," I quieted the room, "one more thing before we get into the details." They looked at me as if I was about to give them more bad news. "Today, I would like you guys to change the way you look at your braking system. I know there are about a hundred parts in the assembly and you know these parts intimately after you spent designing and redesigning them over the years. However, I want you instead to look at the braking system in terms of the functions that it performs per customer requirements. So, instead of thinking about the ECU Housing, think of why we have a Housing, what is its purpose?"

"It's to hold the PCBA, the board with all the electronic components," spoke up Donaldson. "How else would you do it?"

"Exactly!" I bellowed. "How else would you do it? Thank you, Josh. This is exactly the question we'll be asking a lot today." Donaldson and others looked at me as if caught in a trap. I have seen that look before, and it meant that their brains were awakened and shifting focus. Not everyone got it or would ever get it, but I only needed a few converts to lead this group.

"Before we answer that question for the housing," I continued, "let me ask you, what functions does your customer require your braking system to perform?"

"To stop the car," someone shouted out and the room erupted in laughter.

"Perfect!" I shouted, surprising them again. "You can have giant feet stick out to the ground to stop the car like in the Flintstones or you can drive your car into a tree to stop it, but how does your system do it exactly?"

"By applying pulsating pressure on the brake line that in turn pushes and releases the brake pads against the rotors which in turn stops the wheels," said Donaldson.

"Exactly right. So what your system does is apply and pulsate the brake line pressure, correct?" They all nodded in agreement. "That's a function that your brake system performs, apply and pulsate the brake line pressure. What other functions is it required to perform?"

We spent another half hour throwing out various functions that the braking system was performing. I wrote them all out on a white board.

Apply pressure
Pulsate pressure
Control pressure
Attach to vehicle
Sustain protection against environment
Hold PCBA
Maintain performance for 10 years

It was a short list and not perfect, but we did not have much more time to dig into it. Ideally, we would have come up with a FAST diagram to define all the basic and secondary functions and subfunctions, but that normally took a day in itself under normal circumstances.

"Now," I continued, "let's pick 'hold PCBA' function. Yes, we need to have a PCBA with all the electronic components on it so that we can control the pressure and we somehow need to hold that PCBA in place inside the unit. The question is, how else can we hold the PCBA?" I picked up a torn down housing and PCBA and placed them on our conference room table. The PCBA was a flipped board with three boards and many small and large electronic components with three different heat sinks, while the housing was a fairly simple plastic box with some connector pins over molded inside of it and no other electronic components attached. "How else can we hold the PCBA or the electronics inside the unit?" I repeated.

A purchasing manager named Carmen Lee raised her hand to speak, but she only spoke after I nodded in agreement. "It would be nice if we could eliminate the flipped board. I only have one supplier that can make it which leaves me with no leverage. My other suppliers tell me that our competitors use compliant pins to connect multiple boards to the housing and they install some larger electronic components to the housing instead of the boards which they say is easier."

"You can probably eliminate some of the heat sinks that way because you wouldn't have to dissipate as much heat from the board," spoke up one of the engineers quietly.

"But we've always used the flipped board design. Tim Meadows himself designed that concept. He even got a patent for that," said Donaldson.

That was an interesting piece of information. It explained why Meadows was so defensive about changing designs. It was a matter of pride. I was questioning not just the brake system design, but one that he developed himself. It was his baby, and I was calling it ugly.

"Guys, that's a great suggestion. Thank you, Carmen. Everything is up for discussion. I'm sure Tim himself would support it if it meant saving the Volta business." I didn't quite believe that as I said it and others seemed skeptical as well. I quickly walked over to the white board and wrote down:

Cost Reduction Ideas:

(1) Change to stacked board design with compliant pin connections.

(2) Attach some electronic components to the housing, instead of the board.

I was often accused of not adding value as a consultant because I just took ideas that already existed, but this was exactly the goal of a workshop, to bring all the scattered, discarded, untold ideas, and piece them together into a workable plan. Most of the people in this room probably already knew that a stacked board design was an alternative, but they did not even consider it as an option, because it was part of their mental scotoma or their inability to see it as an option due to various things blocking it from consideration. In this case, the main block was probably just fear of displeasing Meadows.

"Speaking of the heat sinks, can we eliminate them altogether?" I continued.

"The heat sinks are a conduit to move heat to the aluminum cover which then dissipates heat to the environment, so we can't remove the heat sinks," responded Donaldson.

"So the function here that we need the system to perform is dissipate heat, correct? The question again is, how can we do it differently?" I challenged the team again.

Nobody responded, and the room fell into silence. I let it stand there for a while, letting the team process my request. Nevertheless, I knew that the team's mind was still restricted by their own design that they knew so well. In fact, they knew it so well that they could not think of anything else as an alternative. Heat sinks were the most common method of dissipating heat in electronics, and we would now need to innovate and find a solution that maybe nobody, including me, has ever seen before. This is where my TRIZ training came in handy. Developed by a Russian scientist, Genrich Altshuller, this method offered 40 solutions to pre-existing and common problems in engineering design. One of them was to use something that already existed in the system or environment to perform a function.

"Is there anything in this braking system or around it that can be used to dissipate heat?" I suggested. They stared at me blankly. I could tell that the hamster wheels in their heads were starting to turn, but needed a little bit more of an assistance. "How about air? There's plenty of air all around the braking system. Or the brake fluid? It's being pumped in and out of the system constantly, couldn't it carry the heat out?"

Donaldson looked at me funny and spoke, "We'll probably have to still keep one of the heat sinks, but we can connect it to the aluminum block instead, which can dissipate heat. Plus, the brake fluid can move the heat out with the existing pump. Then we can change the cover from aluminum to plastic since we won't need it to dissipate heat."

"That's too radical," spoke up another engineer. "It's never been done before."

"It's as radical as the idea that we need to take twenty four dollars out of the design," I retorted. "This is exactly the type of ideas that we need."

"What if we're not able to implement it in time?" asked Donaldson.

"Then it would be the same as if we never tried, we'll lose the Volta business. At least this gives us a shot."

"But Volta will not agree to take such a risk on this design," pushed Donaldson.

"They've trusted you before, haven't they? At one point, your current design was a new design. They trusted you then and they should trust you now."

There were no more questions, so I wrote on the white board.

(3) Dissipate heat using AL block and brake fluid to eliminate aluminum cover.

We continued with this exercise for the next couple of hours. Using my training in functional analysis and TRIZ, I guided the team in challenging their scotomas to find alternatives to performing the required functions. This was a type of guided brainstorming, and it resulted in a list of 50 ideas that we boiled down to 32 as most feasible and worthwhile.

After a quick lunch, it was time to evaluate the ideas. We split up into four teams, each with an engineer, buyer, and cost estimator, then each team was given eight ideas to develop in as much detail as possible. The task was to develop a rough description of a proposed solution and the cost impact and investment needed to execute the idea.

I was pleasantly surprised to see that each team went after it with eagerness. This was the most interactive part of the exercise, and the level of collaboration was tremendous. By now, every person in the room realized the importance of what we were doing and saw that it was possible to get it done. They all put their skepticism behind them, at least for the moment, and were excited to contribute to the solution.

Around 3:00 PM, the teams were ready to present their idea evaluations. This gave us an hour before these were to be presented to Meadows, Rodriguez, and also our surprise guests, still unknown to the team, Bill Rasor and Jim Miller. The stakes were high, and we needed the top management to be aligned before proceeding to implementation.

The first idea that we reviewed was the stacked board design concept. Donaldson led that team and he now projected it on the screen (see Table 2.4).

"Unfortunately, the payback is more than a year, so this would be rejected by Tim," Donaldson announced.

"Wait," I interrupted. "Why does the payback have to be one year?"

Donaldson looked around the room looking for support. "I don't know, it's just how we've always done it."

"There it is again, 'because that's how we've always done it.' That doesn't make it right, does it? Pretend for a minute that you owned Electronica and this investment idea came in front of you. Spend $1,610,000, but make $5,500,000. Would you do it?"

"Hell yes," said one of the buyers.

"If you put it that way, that's a great deal actually," confirmed Donaldson.

"You bet it's a great idea," I agreed. "But what if I told you that you didn't have to invest two million to do it like you assumed in your business case?"

"But that's how much it will cost us to develop and test the new design," Donaldson now was confused.

"Why? Will you have to hire more engineers and buy more testing equipment?" I asked. I got only blank stares, so I continued, "No, you won't have to. All the engineers and equipment are already here and we're already paying for it. The only investment you'll have to make is some test fixtures, which don't cost very much."

The team was not willing to disagree with me on the basis that "it's always been done that way," so Donaldson made a quick estimate of the testing fixtures and updated the calculation (see Table 2.5).

Table 2.4 Stacked board cost reduction proposal

Program	Volta	Volume Years	1,000,000 5
Idea description:	change from flipped board design to stacked board design		
Remove:			Add:
Flipped board PCB	$ (6.78)		Two regular PCBs	$ 5.87
<-- two sets of boards per panel due to milled material needed between boards			<-- three sets of boards per panel due to better panel utilization	
Overmolded pins	$ (0.95)		Compliant pins	$ 1.25
Overmolding process	$ (0.75)		Press in of pins	$ 0.25
TOTAL	$ (8.48)		TOTAL	$ 7.37
TOTAL (DECREASE) / INCREASE	$ (1.11)	per assembly	
ANNUAL (DECREASE) / INCREASE	$ (1,110,000)	per year	
LIFETIME (DECREASE) / INCREASE	$ (5,550,000)	per program	
Reduce investment:			Increase investment:
Board milling	$ (50,000)		Press in tool	$ 20,000
Custom pins	$ (110,000)		Development and Testing	$ 2,000,000
Overmolding tool/fixtures	$ (250,000)			
TOTAL	$ (410,000)		TOTAL	$ 2,020,000
TOTAL INVESTMENT	$ 1,610,000 per program		
PAYBACK	1.45 years		

Table 2.5 *Stacked board cost reduction proposal—MODIFIED*

Program	Volta	Volume Years	1,000,000 5
Idea description:	change from flipped board design to stacked board design		
Remove:			Add:
Flipped board PCB	$ (6.78)	Two regular PCBs	$ 5.87
<-- two sets of boards per panel due to milled material needed between boards		<-- three sets of boards per panel due to better panel utilization	
Overmolded pins	$ (0.95)	Compliant pins	$ 1.25
Overmolding process	$ (0.75)	Press in of pins	$ 0.25
TOTAL	$ (8.48)	TOTAL	$ 7.37
TOTAL (DECREASE) / INCREASE	**$ (1.11)**	**per assembly**	
ANNUAL (DECREASE) / INCREASE	**$ (1,110,000)**	**per year**	
LIFETIME (DECREASE) / INCREASE	**$ (5,550,000)**	**per program**	
Reduce investment:			Increase investment:
Board milling	$ (50,000)	Press in tool	$ 20,000
Custom pins	$ (110,000)	Development and Testing	$ 35,000
Overmolding tool/fixtures	$ (250,000)		
TOTAL	$ (410,000)	TOTAL	$ 55,000
TOTAL INVESTMENT	**$ 355,000 per program**		
PAYBACK	**-0.32 years**		

Suddenly, an idea that was already attractive became dramatically more so. Instead of a payback of almost 1.5 years, now the investment could be paid off within four months. The results might have been different if we contemplated this idea after the product went into production, because then all the tools would already be made and the original investment would have been wasted, but we were only in concept stage, and very little investment has been made so far.

We spent the remaining hour doing similar reviews for the other 31 ideas and were ready now to present to the executives. We even had 10 minutes to spare and took advantage by devouring some pastries that Emily had brought in.

Jim Miller popped in the door first, brimming with excitement and ready to see the results of our workshop. Rasor, Meadows, and Rodriguez arrived shortly after, still showing skepticism in their body language.

"Great to have you all here, gentlemen," I announced. "It's been a crazy day today, lots of work, lots of brain activity, but the team did an amazing job. I'm very proud of their effort and I think you will be also after you see the results."

I now projected the summary slide on a wall screen (see Figure 2.1).

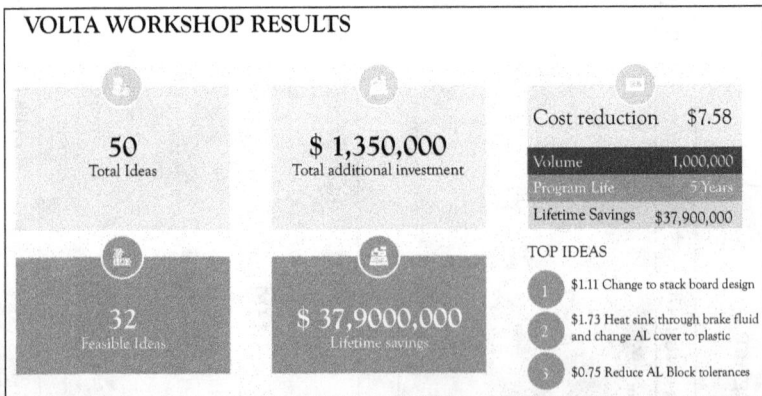

VOLTA WORKSHOP RESULTS

50 Total Ideas	**$ 1,350,000** Total additional investment	Cost reduction $7.58
		Volume 1,000,000
		Program Life 5 Years
		Lifetime Savings $37,900,000
32 Feasible Ideas	**$ 37,9000,000** Lifetime savings	TOP IDEAS
		1 $1.11 Change to stack board design
		2 $1.73 Heat sink through brake fluid and change AL cover to plastic
		3 $0.75 Reduce AL Block tolerances

Figure 2.1 Volta cost reduction workshop results

"Wow!" said Jim Miller after a few moments. "Almost thirty-eight million in program savings?" He seemed excited yet skeptical at the same time.

"We were actually looking for a lot more, twenty-four dollars in piece cost reductions instead of seven and a half that we found, but it's a significant step forward. We'll review all the ideas in detail, but the key to all of them is that they are absolutely feasible to implement. These are not some pie in the sky ideas, we eliminated those already. These are all workable."

"Great! Let's see the details then," said Jim.

We spent more than an hour going through the ideas. The executives seemed impressed with the level of detail that the team generated, but only Jim seemed truly excited about the potential. Meadows mostly just stared at the screen without showing much emotion. Considering that he always looked that way, I could not tell if he was buying into it or not.

"Well, thank you very much," I said when the presentation was over. "The team did an incredible job in such a short period of time. It's obvious that everyone in this room understands the importance of what we're trying to accomplish. This was a great first step. The next challenge that awaits us is implementation and that starts next week already. So, please have a great weekend, recharge your batteries, and be ready on Monday to roll up your sleeves and grind this out."

The team was thanked by other executives on their way out. I also thanked the executives for their support as they left. Only Jim stayed behind.

"Great job, Doug," he said. "You look like you need some rest. Can I buy you dinner?"

"Thank you, but I think I'll just go straight to bed tonight. It's been a long couple of weeks."

"Suit yourself. I'm flying back home tomorrow morning, so good luck next week, but call me if you run into any trouble."

"I'll be fine. Just make sure Meadows works on implementing all those ideas," I said.

He waved good bye and was out the door leaving me all alone with the conference room full of brake parts, printouts, and white boards full of colorful writing. It was now suddenly quiet, and I felt alone again. Then, it hit me, I had an even bigger day tomorrow.

Saturday, Day 13 of 28

I had the whole day to prepare for my date with Emily, but I felt panicked. I have not been out on a date with anyone other than my ex-wife in 20 years. I was not thinking of that when I asked Emily out, but the realization was now here, and I had a lot of scenarios running through my head on ways in which Emily would reject me. No matter what lines I came up with to charm her, somehow the conversation in my head always eventually led to me saying something stupid and me ending up alone for the rest of my life.

I came down to the hotel restaurant for breakfast and was again greeted by Omar and Stephanie. "Do you guys work here seven days a week?" I asked Stephanie jokingly.

"Yes," she said with her usual smile, but very matter of fact. She placed my usual coffee and orange juice on the table.

"Oh," I replied embarrassed. "They don't give you any days to relax?"

"I'm only here five hours every morning, so I can only get to about thirty five hours a week, which is barely enough to pay the bills."

"Sorry," I said clumsily, "they probably don't pay you much in this place."

"That's all right." Her mood seemed unaffected by my stupid questions. "I pick up bartending hours at Ducky's on Fridays and Saturdays. That's what really pays for my school."

"No kidding. I'm going there tonight."

"Really? What's the occasion?" she said and watched my face turn red like a little boy. "Oh, I get it, you have a date." She laughed when I did not protest.

A thought suddenly crossed my mind. "Say, you probably know how to use a computer, right?"

"Of course," she replied with a confused look on her face.

"Do you know how to use Outlook and Excel and all the other software?"

"Yes, I've been using those since high school. Doesn't everybody?"

"Sorry, I forgot that you're a millennial. You guys were born with phones and laptops," I replied. "In that case, how would you like a job with Electronica?"

Her smile disappeared, and she suddenly became very serious. "Are you messing with me?" she said.

"No, I'm serious. I need an admin and I think you would be perfect." I announced with confidence. Stephanie's face was now agape staring at me, so I continued, "In fact, since you'll be at Ducky's tonight, I can introduce you to my previous admin. She will probably be the one training you next week while I'm out of town."

"Next week?" she said, still in shock.

"Yes, I need someone right away. Is that all right?"

"Yes, but I'd have to quit here," she started to come to it. "How much does it pay?"

I scratched my head, realizing that this is information that I didn't have. "Right. That's a good question. We can settle that later tonight when I see you at the Ducky's. I'll make sure it's better than what you make here. Plus, it would be five days a week, so you'd have some free time on the weekends."

"Thank you, Doug," she said with a smile back on her face. "This means a lot to me."

"Don't thank me yet. Before you make a final decision, you might want to consider the fact that you'll have to deal with me all day now instead of just at breakfast."

She laughed. "I look forward to it."

* * *

It was 5:45 PM on my car clock. I have been waiting in my car parked outside of Ducky's, a pleasant beige building with blue shutters, since 5:30 PM and spent most of that time dreading 6:00 PM. I left my hotel early in case I got lost on my way to the restaurant, which happened to be only five minutes away, so I ended up sitting in my car waiting and sweating in my freshly dry cleaned suit. I do not ever recall being this nervous about anything, not even on my wedding night.

I got out of my car and walked inside the restaurant. "I have a 6:00 PM reservation for Doug," I said to the hostess.

"Yes," she smiled. "Emily is already waiting for you."

"What?" I spat out in shock.

"Follow me, please," she replied calmly.

The hostess led me through the restaurant, which was very nice. The décor was elegant, but not too fancy. The atmosphere seemed casual and the crowd mature.

"Hello, Emily," I said when the hostess dropped me off at a booth in the back of the restaurant where Emily was seated. She was wearing a gorgeous blue dress that took my breath away.

"Hi, Doug," she said without getting up. "Are you planning to sit down?"

I woke up from my trance and sat down across from her. "Sorry. You look beautiful," I said. "I apologize, I got a bit mesmerized there for a second."

She smiled. "Thank you."

"I'm also a bit surprised you're already here and that I got such a great table," I admitted.

"You didn't. I had us upgraded."

I was puzzled. "How did you manage that?"

"Electronica does a lot of business with Ducky's. I call them at least twice a week to make reservations and Bill orders his lunch here every day."

"Oh, right, that makes sense."

A waiter came by with some water. "Your steaks will be ready in about ten minutes, Ms. Emily," he said and walked away.

"You ordered for me already?" I said in mild shock. I was not sure if I should take it as a compliment or a hit to my ego.

"It's the best thing that they have here and I confirmed with Jim that you like steak," she replied without skipping a beat.

"Jim knows that you're here with me?"

"He's the one that convinced me to agree to the date if you ever had the nerve to ask," she said smiling.

I pulled on my tie nervously trying to find a way to hang myself. "Jim, Jim, Jim," is all I could think of to say.

"Don't feel too bad. Jim was a good friend to do that, but I would have said yes anyway."

I finally smiled back and relaxed a bit. "I'm glad you said yes," I said. I opened the menu out of habit and located the steak section.

"They are $35 each," she threw out as if she could read my mind. I was starting to think that maybe she was psychic because she was way ahead of me on everything since I have met her. "But, I know the owner pretty well, so it's on the house tonight."

"Oh no you don't, I'm paying for dinner tonight." I had to draw the line somewhere before all of my testosterone evaporated.

"I'm sure the waiter will appreciate it," she said trying not to laugh.

"I hope you don't think I'm cheap or anything?" I was still regretting looking up steak prices in the menu. "It's a force of habit as a cost engineer, I'm always trying to figure out what things cost."

"You mean you're trying to figure out how much food should cost?" she asked.

"Again, it's not about being cheap," I reassured her. "I'm just curious."

"So how much should this steak cost?"

I shook my head. "No way, I'm not going to tell you what goes on inside my head. You'll think I'm the biggest dork in the world and a bore to boot."

"No, I insist," she said.

"Ok, if you insist," I hesitated. This could easily end our first date early, but I felt like I would not be able to keep any secrets from her anyway, so I might as well let her inside my head. "First of all, the price for the steak is not based on its cost, but on what people in this area are willing to pay for a certain quality of steak. The market determines the price." She nodded her head indicating that she was with me so far. "So," I continued, "the question for the owner of a restaurant really becomes, how do I make a steak at a cost below $35 so I can still make money?"

"That's fascinating," Emily interrupted, and I still could not tell whether she meant it or if she was being sarcastic. "And how would the owner know the cost of making the steak?"

"Great question. One might say that it's a simple matter of how much he has to pay for the raw meat, which could be fifteen to twenty-five dollars per pound depending on the cut, then throwing some markup on top of it to get to a price. A lot of experts in the restaurant business would say that you need to have at least fifty percent markup on your raw material cost to cover all the expenses and profit." I kept looking at Emily to make sure I was not losing her, but she kept staring at me as if she was interested in what I was saying, so I went on. "However, the way I look at the restaurant is as if it was a factory, which it really is. It manufactures food for customers that happen to be right here to eat it. So, not only do you have the cost of labor, equipment, and overhead to manufacture the food, but also the cost to deliver the food to the customer, which is the waiter, the tables, and all the overhead that goes along with that. Are you sure you want me to continue?" I stopped to make sure I did not lose her.

She laughed. "Please do, I really find this fascinating. So, if there's something wrong with you for thinking like this, then maybe there's something wrong with me also, because I'm enjoying this very much."

"Ok, but just remember you asked for it, not me." She laughed again, so I continued. "So, the question now is, how do you know what the cost is of all that to make a steak? If, let's say, the owner paid fifteen dollars for the raw meat, is the remaining twenty dollars enough to cover other costs and profit? Not that he could change the price if he found out that it is not, but then at least he would know that he'd have to do something to reduce the cost in order to make money."

"And how do you figure that out?" she asked with what seemed like real curiosity.

"Well, let's start with labor. If the guy in the kitchen making steaks can produce twenty of them per hour and he makes fifteen bucks per hour, then that's seventy-five cents per steak. Then, you have to pay for the oil or butter used for cooking and the gas used to power the stove and the oven. You can calculate this based on your monthly cost of those and roughly allocating based on usage relative to other equipment in the kitchen. For example, the chef could probably roughly tell you that maybe ten percent of all oil and gas is used on that station. Let's guess that ends up being another dollar of cost for each steak. Then, of course, you have the cost of the equipment itself. If the stove costs ten thousand and it lasts for ten thousand operating hours, then the cost is one dollar per hour or five cents per steak. Then, you have the cost of the maintenance and repair, the cost of the kitchen part of the building, the cost of maintaining an accountant, the cost of a delivery truck that you might need for delivery of various things. All of that might add up to another couple of bucks."

The waiter interrupted me as he brought the steaks to our table. "Enjoy," he said, "and please let me know if you need anything else."

"Then comes the serving cost," I continued when the waiter left. "The waiter probably doesn't get paid much per hour and he serves several tables at a time and many meals per hour, so let's say that's another fifty cents per steak. But, then you have the cost of the building housing the guests and all the tables and accessories. Of course, you also have post processing, which is washing the dishes and garbage bags and garbage pickup. Not to mention the scrap, which is all the food you throw away because you burned it or the customer didn't like it or it spoils because you didn't get to use it. So, I have no idea how much all of that would cost, but I'm sure it adds up to at least ten dollars per steak."

"Wow!" said Emily as she was finishing her steak. "That's a lot to think about just to eat a steak."

I knew she was teasing, and I smiled. "When I'm with you, it doesn't even cross my mind."

She blushed, piercing her normally tough exterior. "What happens when you find out that you're not making any money on steaks?" she deflected the attention from herself.

"Well, you probably still have to serve the steak at the same price, because you need to serve steaks in this type of restaurant. But, you might learn that you're making money on other things that you serve, like pasta or drinks. That's probably why we pay ten dollars for a glass of wine."

As if on demand, Stephanie arrived at our table with two glasses of wine. "Hi, Doug. I didn't know your date was with Ms. Emily," she said.

"You know Emily?" I asked, surprised.

"Of course," she said as if I should have known that, "everyone knows Ms. Emily."

"Well, this will be easier, then," I said. "Emily, I'm planning to hire Stephanie as my admin. I was hoping that you could show her the ropes while I'm out next week."

"It would be my pleasure, Stephanie," said Emily without giving it much thought.

"Thank you, Ms. Emily. I'm looking forward to it," said Stephanie and walked away.

"You made a good choice, Doug. She's a bright young lady," Emily assured me.

"I thought I could use some of her positive energy at the office."

Emily laughed. "Sounds like you're planning to stick around," she said, almost as if she wanted me to verify.

"It depends on how it goes tonight," I said, trying to be funny.

She laughed again, then listened to me talk about various nonsense for another couple of hours. The conversation was so easy flowing that I completely lost track of time.

"I had a really good time," she said finally. "Thank you for asking me out."

"You're leaving already?" I said, surprised.

"Sorry, my boys get into trouble if I leave them alone for too long, so I need to run back."

"Those two teenage boys?" I asked, still not quite sure if she had kids of her own.

"Yes, my sister's kids. She passed away from cancer last year, so I adopted them. Sorry, I have to go," she said and got up to leave.

I stood up as well and reached out for her hand that she extended for a handshake. "I had a great time also, just hope I didn't bore you with my cost engineering stuff."

"Not at all, I like a smart man," she said as she shook my hand. "I'll see you in a week. Good luck on your trip."

I watched her walk away and did not even notice Stephanie standing next to me.

"You picked a good one, Doug. She's a tough cookie," she said startling me.

"You're telling me. She might be the toughest part of this assignment."

CHAPTER 3

The Grind

Monday, Day 15 of 28

I was still thinking about Emily when we left the Charlotte airport in a rental car with Evan and Alex. Did the date go well or not, I wondered? Emily was probably the toughest woman to read that I have ever met. I never felt in control when I was around her. It is as if I was playing chess with Kasparov, she was always five steps ahead of me.

"Thinking about the plant visit?" asked Evan, who sat next to me in a front passenger seat, after I stayed quiet for a while driving the car.

"Yes," I lied.

"Anything you want us to do during our visit?" he asked, and I just realized that I have not given him or Alex any direction at all for this week.

"You just follow my lead and learn, but keep your eyes wide open. You'll be learning just the basics of some manufacturing processes, but you also need to try and build the big picture view of the factory. Meaning that without looking at a plant layout, you should understand the flow of material through the factory, how many people touch it as it moves along in the process, how many people work in every department, what is the capacity utilization of each department, and most importantly what does that mean in terms of cost."

Evan nodded his head in agreement, but I could tell that he did not quite know what I meant. I looked in a rear view mirror to see if Alex understood, but he was staring out the window with his ear buds in.

"Don't worry," I said, "seeing is believing and you guys will understand it much better once on the floor."

We arrived at the plant two hours later. Bud Kulig, our VP of Operations, greeted us in the lobby. He was a hefty man, but carried the weight easily and naturally. He shed his designer suit for khakis and a polo shirt and looked more natural in that outfit. Most manufacturing guys who I have met were very practical and straightforward, probably due to the necessity of having to solve critical problems on a daily basis, and Kulig seemed like that kind of man as well.

"I'm glad you're here, Doug," Kulig said, and I could tell that he meant it. "It would be devastating to the people here if we don't win that Volta business."

"I'm happy to help," I said as we followed him out of the lobby and through the office full of dated cubicle furniture. It looked like the furniture was original from when they built this factory probably a few decades ago.

Kulig seemed to detect my disdain and said, "It's not much, but it's home. I haven't had much money to refresh this place, but we find it cozy."

"Don't worry about us, we're not here to judge your decorations," I assured him.

We arrived at a conference room, and they really could have used an interior decorator, because none of the furniture matched. There was a gray table in the middle, but it was surrounded by chairs of four different colors and styles, a hodgepodge pulled together over time, and green walls covered with red Electronica posters. It was a lot for the eyes to take in, and I had to squint to get used to the environment.

"My controller, Dave Porter, will be here in a few minutes," said Kulig. "Per your request, he reserved today and tomorrow for your visit. We also scheduled a plant tour this morning with my plant manager."

"That's perfect. Thank you, Bud," I said.

As we settled in the conference room, both Dave Porter and the plant manager, Andy Rollins, joined us. Porter was a short man with a quiet demeanor, while Rollins had his sleeves rolled up and a demeanor of a bulldog. After some introductions, we got straight into it.

"Here's our P&L for last year, as you requested," said Porter and projected an Excel summary on the screen (see Table 3.1).

Table 3.1 Electronica plant P&L

	Jan	Feb	Mar	Apr	May	Jun	Jul	Aug	Sep	Oct	Nov	Dec	TOTAL
Sales	25,216,942	25,216,960	25,216,942	25,216,942	25,216,960	25,216,848	25,216,942	25,216,960	25,248,155	25,248,191	25,248,155	25,248,155	302,728,056
Material	19,518,758	19,523,723	19,556,230	19,548,512	19,598,458	19,523,874	19,495,821	19,659,751	19,654,789	19,678,325	19,587,456	19,375,234	234,720,931
Direct labor	146,329	132,911	146,329	146,329	132,911	146,329	146,329	132,911	146,329	146,329	132,911	146,329	1,702,277
Direct laborfringes	90,905	91,530	91,530	90,905	91,530	91,905	91,127	91,308	91,905	91,349	91,308	91,127	1,096,429
Hourly cost	237,234	224,441	237,859	237,234	224,441	238,234	237,456	224,219	238,234	237,678	224,219	237,456	2,798,706
Indirect labor	92,650	92,650	92,650	92,650	92,650	92,650	92,650	92,650	92,650	92,650	92,650	92,650	1,111,795
Indirect laborfringes	31,852	31,852	31,852	31,852	31,852	31,852	31,852	31,852	31,852	31,852	31,852	31,852	382,224
	124,502	124,502	124,502	124,502	124,502	124,502	124,502	124,502	124,502	124,502	124,502	124,502	1,494,019
Rent	245,120	224,320	224,320	224,320	224,320	224,320	224,320	224,320	224,320	224,320	224,320	224,320	2,712,640
Utilities	61,600	49,600	61,600	61,600	49,600	61,600	61,600	49,600	61,600	61,600	49,600	61,600	691,200
Depreciation and amortization	346,667	346,667	346,667	346,667	346,667	346,667	346,667	346,667	346,667	346,667	346,667	346,667	4,160,000
Maintenance	206,200	162,750	78,750	114,300	203,000	73,750	101,700	245,000	24,500	134,800	84,750	11,000	1,440,500
Insurance	25,000	25,000	25,000	25,000	25,000	25,000	25,000	25,000	25,000	25,000	25,000	25,000	300,000
Package, indirect, and perishables	7,012	9,500	3,354	3,112	5,520	3,104	3,362	4,820	5,815	6,312	5,065	3,109	60,083

Table 3.1 Electronica plant P&L (Continued)

	Jan	Feb	Mar	Apr	May	Jun	Jul	Aug	Sep	Oct	Nov	Dec	TOTAL
Brokers, diesel, tolls, and freights	34,835	34,099	37,044	34,835	37,044	34,590	36,062	36,430	35,449	34,712	35,694	35,326	426,119
Lean mfg. and shingo	7,500	7,500	7,500	7,500	7,500	7,500	7,500	7,500	7,500	7,500	7,500	7,500	90,000
Others	62,332	42,672	23,177	36,260	32,692	23,560	24,515	20,212	19,181	30,880	56,672	42,110	414,263
Total manufacturing expenses	996,266	902,107	807,411	853,594	931,342	800,090	830,726	959,548	750,031	871,791	835,267	756,631	10,294,805
Salaries	280,628	318,848	280,628	280,628	318,848	280,628	280,628	318,848	280,628	280,628	318,848	280,628	3,520,414
Salaries-fringes	88,639	86,584	85,318	85,420	92,813	85,420	83,732	92,692	85,420	77,689	87,263	83,732	1,034,721
	369,267	405,432	365,946	366,047	411,661	366,047	364,360	411,540	366,047	358,317	406,111	364,360	4,555,135
Telephones and Internet	10,000	10,000	10,000	10,000	10,000	10,000	10,000	10,000	10,000	10,000	10,000	10,000	120,000
Office and cleaning Supplies	10,000	10,000	10,000	10,000	10,000	10,000	10,000	10,000	10,000	10,000	10,000	10,000	120,000
Travel	2,300	1,500	700	967	3,986	239	2,332	5,689	569	345	1,235	3,490	23,352
Professional services	75,226	74,382	74,101	72,532	73,424	71,506	72,324	80,718	71,948	71,154	71,948	71,154	880,416
Others	107,397	72,344	91,498	32,818	52,318	32,526	58,526	32,526	90,926	32,426	90,926	38,926	733,153
Total plant overhead	204,922	168,226	186,299	126,316	149,727	124,270	153,182	138,933	183,443	123,925	184,109	133,570	1,876,922
Total expenses	21,450,949	21,348,431	21,278,246	21,256,206	21,440,131	21,177,018	21,206,046	21,518,492	21,317,046	21,394,538	21,361,663	20,991,753	255,740,519
Grossprofit	3,765,993	3,868,530	3,938,602	3,960,736	3,776,830	4,039,830	4,010,895	3,698,468	3,931,109	3,853,653	3,886,491	4,256,402	46,987,538

We all stared at it for a while. I saw that Evan and Alex were looking at it, but I could tell that they had no idea what they were looking at.

"Do you have this split up by departments or products?" I asked. "I'm curious about how you develop your overhead rates."

"We actually use only one rate for the whole plant," stated Porter, happy to make it easy for me.

"One rate for the whole plant?" I asked to confirm.

"Yes, our overhead cost is 500% of labor cost, so whenever we quote business, we just use the same five to one ratio," explained Porter.

I checked the quote sheet that I got from Mark Harrington (see Table 1.1) and sure enough the plant overhead was five times the labor cost. "So, what is in your labor and overhead costs?" I asked.

"Labor is all the direct people on the assembly lines and their fringe benefits, then overhead is everything else except for depreciation," answered Porter.

"And what do you mean by everything?"

"Everything, everything," said Parker, a bit irritated. "Indirect labor, which is all the line leads, technicians, manufacturing and quality engineers on the floor, plus all the material handlers, warehouse guys, warehousing itself, electricity for the whole building, the building rental cost, and on and on. Like I said, everything."

"And you're just tracking total plant cost?" I asked.

"Well, actually we separate our automotive and appliance businesses," said Porter simply.

I looked at him for a moment, dumbfounded. "What appliance business?" I finally said. "Nobody has mentioned anything to me about an appliance business."

"Really?" asked Kulig. "It's the only thing keeping us afloat."

"You mean, you're making appliance parts in this building?" I said to confirm what I was hearing.

"Yes, we've been doing it for years," said Kulig and chuckled. "We make pumps for refrigerators that have a very similar

Table 3.2 Electronica plant P&L

	Brakes-current		Appliance-current		Total-current	
Sales	$135,000,000		$167,000,000		$302,000,000	
Material	$110,100,000	81.6%	$124,640,000	74.6%	$234,740,000	77.7%
Labor	$1,120,000	0.8%	$1,680,000	1.0%	$2,800,000	0.9%
Overhead	$5,500,000	4.1%	$8,400,000	5.0%	$13,900,000	4.6%
Depreciation	$2,080,000	1.5%	$2,080,000	1.2%	$4,160,000	1.4%
SG&A	$13,500,000	10.0%	$16,700,000	10.0%	$30,200,000	10.0%
Profit	$2,700,000	2.0%	$13,500,000	8.1%	$16,200,000	5.4%

manufacturing process to the braking system. We do SMT, where we surface mount the electronic components on the board, and final assembly for both."

"Could you please show me a breakdown between those two businesses?" I asked Porter.

"Sure," said Porter and projected a summary (see Table 3.2).

"As you can see, we make good money on the appliance business, over eight percent," said Kulig, "but we're only two percent on the automotive business and declining without any new programs won."

"Very interesting," I said. "Would it be possible to see the plant layout before we go out there?"

"Sure," said Andy Rollins, the plant manager, "we have it on the wall here." He walked over to the back wall and pulled a printout off of it, then laid it out on the conference room table (see Figure 3.1).

"As you can see, we have two SMT lines and two assembly lines dedicated to each business," continued Porter. "We currently produce about one million units for each business, but we have a bunch of appliance programs and only a couple of brakes programs."

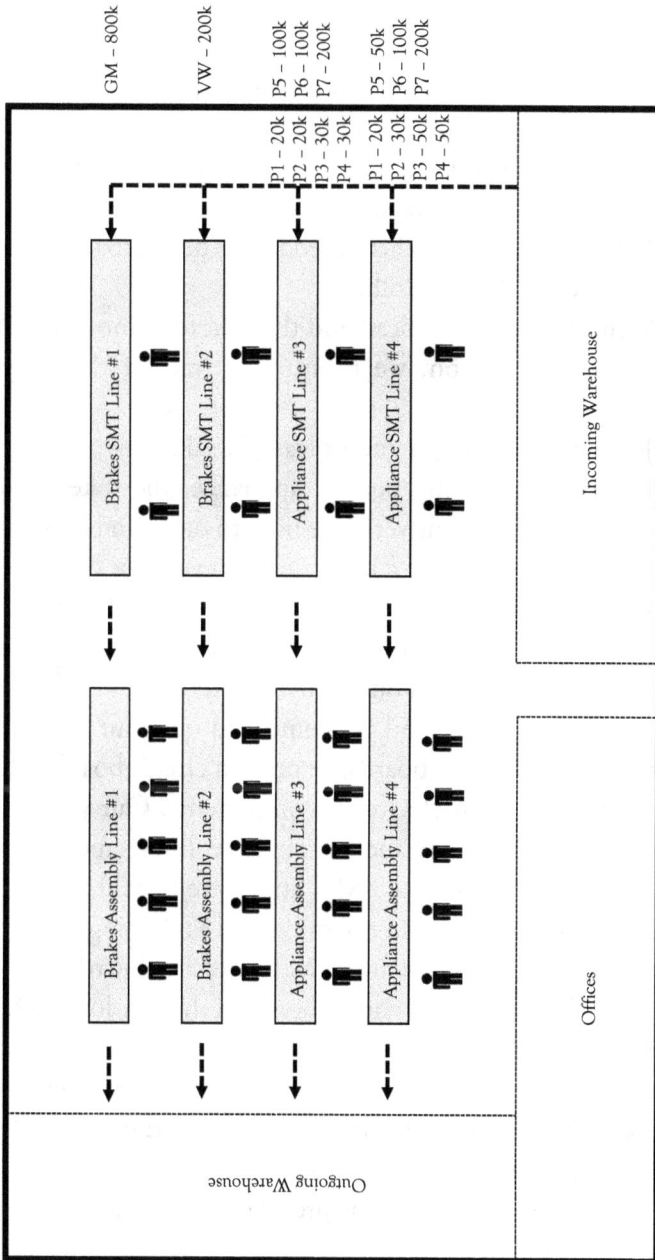

Figure 3.1 Electronica plant layout

"Perfect," I announced. "Let's get on the floor and walk through it."

* * *

We started the plant tour in the incoming warehouse. As we walked through the rows and rows of ceiling high storage racks, I noticed that there was a lot of activity in one portion of the warehouse, but very little in others.

"What percentage of this warehouse is dedicated to the appliance business?" I asked Rollins.

Rollins scratched his head and thought for a moment. "Well, that's a good question, we really don't track it that way," he admitted.

"Just give me a rough guess please," I said.

"I would say seventy percent appliance," he stated and was surprised by his own answer. "We have to order and hold a lot of material because there are a lot of different versions of the designs and they are made only so often. Automotive, on the other hand, is more high volume and just one or two consistent designs, so we move the material in and out pretty quickly."

I nodded my head and we continued our tour to the SMT lines. This is where the boards, or printed circuit boards (PCBs), were populated with electronic components. Our group stood between the appliance and automotive lines, and I noticed quickly that the appliance SMT lines were both down. I interrupted Rollins, who was in the middle of explaining the process, "How come the two appliance SMT lines are down?"

"Oh, it's nothing to worry about, we have a lot of change-overs on those lines because of the many programs and designs within the programs," he explained. "The lines will be running as soon as we change over the materials and the pick and place software program."

"So your efficiency must be pretty low on the appliance business?" I stated.

"Actually, our efficiency on these is almost a hundred percent, because we have people that help us run through the breaks.

Otherwise, we'd run out of capacity and would have to run on the weekends. We already run three shifts twenty four hours per day and five days a week."

I was confused. "So what do you include in your efficiency calculation?"

"Just planned and unplanned downtime, but not setup or changeover times."

"So how do you account for changeover?" I asked.

"I don't," he admitted. "I guess it's in overhead somewhere. You'd have to ask Porter."

"What about your efficiency on the automotive lines?"

"Those are about eighty five percent. We run three shifts on one line with some open capacity and only one on the other, so we don't need to work during breaks or lunches."

"How about your changeovers on the automotive lines?" I said.

"We actually don't really change over, because each line only runs one program. There is one changeover on the GM program, but we only do it once per week, so it doesn't really slow us down much."

I nodded my head, and he continued to walk us through the processes. Evan and Alex were hanging on to Rollins's every word. This was all new to them, and they were writing everything down as I instructed them prior to the visit.

Rollins explained the final assembly process, and it seemed that it was a very similar situation as far as differences between automotive and appliance business. There was a lot of idle time on the appliance side, as workers were either changing over or their line was starved by the SMT lines because those were changing over. On the other hand, the two automotive lines seemed to be running smoothly without interruptions.

"What is the capacity utilization of all the lines?" I asked.

"They are all fully utilized today," answered Rollins.

"But your plant layout showed only two hundred thousand pieces produced on line two?" I said, puzzled.

Rollins seemed confused about my questioning. "Correct, but we only run one shift on that machine, so it's fully utilized on that shift."

Now I was confused. "I guess let me ask a different way. Out of the total 120 hours that are available per week, how many hours is each line actually running and producing parts?"

Rollins looked around as if searching for someone or something to answer my question. "We don't really track that, but I can have something put together for you when we get back to the office."

"Perfect," I said. "And let me ask you, which part of the business takes up most of yours and your staff's time? Roughly, what percentage of time do you spend on appliance side and what percentage on automotive side?"

"I would say easily 70% on the appliance side, there are just a lot of programs and the customers are picky about what they want us to produce and when. My accounting guys always have issues with invoices and getting paid on time, plus we're constantly fighting to procure the materials needed for various versions of the designs. And my manufacturing guys are always tweaking the software programs on those machines, going back and forth between different designs. So, yes, easily 70%, if not more."

"That makes sense," I agreed. "And, one more question, if you don't mind. Which lines were you assuming to use for the Volta business?"

"Actually, we were assuming a brand new line that we were planning to squeeze inside this building."

"You can't use the existing lines?" I asked.

"Yes, we could, but it would require a major remodeling of the lines. It's a lot easier just to buy a new one."

I nodded and indicated that we can move on. Rollins led us to the outgoing inventory warehouse next. Similar to the incoming warehouse, portions of the warehouse seemed very busy, while others seemed idle and dark. I also noticed a lot of dunnage stored on the rack shelves, mostly in the form of large plastic trays, about 10 per pallet.

"What is all the dunnage for?" I asked Rollins.

"That's a pain actually," he said and shook his head. "There are hundreds of design versions for the appliance business and each of them has a different dunnage tray design, so we must keep those around until the customers are ready to produce those designs. Plus, we have to wash these constantly, because the customer doesn't want even a spec of dirt to get on their appliances."

"So, what portion of this warehouse would you say is dedicated to the appliance business?" I asked.

"Probably about 70%," said Rollins.

I nodded, and he continued to explain the warehouse to Evan and Alex. After the warehouse, Rollins took us through the test lab where they tested a certain number of parts per day, which did not seem too extensive. It was back to the office after that where lunch was already waiting for us in the conference room.

* * *

"Here is the summary of capacity utilization for each line," said Rollins and handed me a piece of paper (see Table 3.3) as we were finishing lunch. "The SMT and final assembly are basically synchronized, so this is for both combined."

Table 3.3 Capacity utilization of each line

	Capacity utilization
Line 1	80%
Line 2	20%
Line 3	50%
Line 4	50%

"Thank you," I said and stared at the piece of paper. It all was starting to make a lot of sense now. However, we spent the rest of the afternoon going through the numbers in detail with the controller. I wanted to make sure that Evan and Alex got a full picture of the plant and understood what all the numbers meant and where they came from. "So, do you see the problem here?" I asked them when we were alone in the room.

They both had that deer-in-headlights look on their faces. I stared back and waited until finally Evan spoke up with hesitation. "I mean… the automotive business is not making enough money because the lines are underutilized."

"How about this?" I proposed. "You guys both think about what the real problem or problems might be and write your solutions to those problems on a piece of paper. You can give me your papers, folded up, tomorrow morning. Then, we'll open those up after we finish up here tomorrow. How does that sound?"

They nodded in agreement. I did not expect good answers, because of their lack of experience evaluating cost structures, but I was hoping to make them think. This was half the battle in training someone.

Tuesday, Day 16 of 28

I felt hung over the next morning after having just a couple of drinks while taking the plant folks out to dinner the night before at a local hot wings place. I have not drank in a long time, so it hit me more than I expected, and the hot sauce did not help either, but it was always good to form personal relationships with the people who you worked with but did not see in person very often. Especially because what I was going to tell them today was going to flip their world upside down. I needed them to be open minded and hearing things from a friend, rather than a stranger, always helped.

Evan and Alex handed me their folded pieces of paper as we drove to the plant. I was tempted to open them, but slid them into my backpack instead.

"Did you guys sleep ok?" I asked them, noticing that they both looked miserable. They shook their heads and I could not help but laugh. "Don't worry," I said, "we only have four more days to go."

Kulig, Porter, and Rollins were already waiting for us in the conference room. Fortunately, so was the freshly brewed pot of coffee.

"Good morning, gentlemen," I said as I helped myself to a cup. "Are you ready to figure this out today?"

"We're curious to hear your thoughts," said Kulig. "We hope you found something that will help us win that Volta business."

I decided to get right into it. "Well, for starters, you make more money on automotive than you think and not as much on appliances."

They seemed surprised. Kulig turned to Porter looking for answers.

"I am pretty confident in our numbers," said Porter.

"No offense, but they are wrong," I stated firmly. "It's not that you are adding things up incorrectly, it's the fact that you chose the wrong method to allocate and distribute cost. The five to one allocation of overhead based on labor is not applicable to this plant. That's because, although the equipment looks similar, your two businesses are very different in how they operate."

"I don't understand," said Kulig. "What are you telling me?"

"Let me show you," I said and projected my computer screen (see Table 3.4).

Table 3.4 Updated Electronica plant P&L

	Brakes-current		Appliance-current		Total-current	
Sales	$135,000,000		$167,000,000		$302,000,000	
Material	$110,100,000	81.6%	$124,640,000	74.6%	$234,740,000	77.7%
Labor	$1,120,000	0.8%	$1,680,000	1.0%	$2,800,000	0.9%
Overhead	$4,170,000	3.1%	$9,730,000	5.8%	$13,900,000	4.6%
Depreciation	$2,080,000	1.5%	$2,080,000	1.2%	$4,160,000	1.4%
SG&A	$11,500,000	8.5%	$18,700,000	11.2%	$30,200,000	10.0%
Profit	$6,030,000	4.5%	$10,170,000	6.1%	$16,200,000	5.4%

"You are currently assigning the same overhead cost to each laborer, regardless of which business they work in, which implies that there is the same overhead effort required for both," I continued. "However, the overhead support on appliances is much greater. For one, 70% of your warehouses are taken up by the appliance business. Then, your salaried staff spends about 70% of their time on the appliance business, and I'm sure the same thing happens at the headquarters. Then, there is the wasted time on the appliance side of the business, where your current uptime is only 50%, so you're paying your people and other resources to stand idle for half the time. We don't have enough time to do a full Activity Based Costing exercise, but I just took the liberty of roughly redistributing your overhead cost based on effort. I allocated 70% of manufacturing overhead and an additional two million dollars of SG&A to the appliance business. So, now, instead of two percent profit, your automotive business is probably closer to four or five percent, and your appliance business is probably closer to six percent instead of eight."

They were still absorbing the numbers, so I kept going. "Now, while your appliance lines are probably not capable of taking on more programs, and thus improving on that profitability, the automotive business can double its output with very little additional cost. That's why I think the Volta business should be quoted on a marginal basis."

"What do you mean on a marginal basis?" interrupted Porter.

"Well, think of the Volta program as a side hustle. You already have your base business and this is just incremental, like a cherry on top. You are already paying for the building and the indirect and salaried staff, so this would be just something extra. Another way to visualize it is imagining what your plant cost structure would look like if I plugged the Volta business in here with only the necessary costs that you would need to run it?"

I showed some additional columns in my spreadsheet with more calculations (see Table 3.5).

Table 3.5 *P&L including Volta business*

	Brakes - current		Appliance - current		Total – current		Volta business		Total - combined		Brakes - combined	
Sales	$135,000,000		$167,000,000		$302,000,000		$100,000,000		$402,000,000		$235,000,000	
Material	$110,100,000	81.6%	$124,640,000	74.6%	$234,740,000	77.7%	$80,000,000	80.0%	$314,740,000	78.3%	$190,100,000	80.9%
Labor	$1,120,000	0.8%	$1,680,000	1.0%	$2,800,000	0.9%	$560,000	0.6%	$3,360,000	0.8%	$1,680,000	0.7%
Overhead	$4,170,000	3.1%	$9,730,000	5.8%	$13,900,000	4.6%	$1,000,000	1.0%	$14,900,000	3.7%	$5,170,000	2.2%
Depreciation	$2,080,000	1.5%	$2,080,000	1.2%	$4,160,000	1.4%	$500,000	0.5%	$4,660,000	1.2%	$2,580,000	1.1%
SG&A	$11,500,000	8.5%	$18,700,000	11.2%	$30,200,000	10.0%	$1,440,000	1.4%	$31,640,000	7.9%	$12,940,000	5.5%
Profit	$6,030,000	4.5%	$10,170,000	6.1%	$16,200,000	5.4%	$16,500,000	16.5%	$32,700,000	8.1%	$22,530,000	9.6%

"As you can see," I continued, "by plugging in the Volta business with just the added cost, but a bunch more revenue, we improve the profitability from 5.4% to 8.1% overall and from 4.5% to 9.6% for the brakes business specifically.

"And my recommendation also is that we consolidate the GM and VW programs on line one, then dedicate line two to the Volta business. It will require a tear up, but I'm guessing it will be half the price of a brand new line, plus it would improve our overall equipment utilization."

"That assumes that we'd have to start up production at 18 seconds like the other programs and have no chance to meet our annual cost improvement goals," pointed out Rollins.

"You don't have to worry about that anymore, Jim Miller will be rolling out new objectives shortly," I assured him. "Plus, the Volta program will take a few months to ramp up, so you'll have time to fine tune the process."

"But your Volta program SG&A is only 1.4% and your overhead to labor ratio is only two," protested Porter. "How is that possible?"

"Yet my overall business profitability with Volta increases from 5.4% to 8.1%, doesn't it?" I countered. "Think of it more in the absolute terms instead of percentages and ratios. For example, if I used your standard 10% SG&A, that would mean an additional ten million dollars per year, even though you're only spending thirty million on SG&A today and you would need very few additional resources to take care of the Volta program. You already have the sales staff, the accountants, the HR people, the IT, the building. Everything is already in place, so why would you need another ten million?"

"And you think we can make 16.5% on the Volta program, even with what it looks like a hundred dollar price per unit?" questioned Kulig.

"We'll have to make that much, because we have to give three percent per year back to Volta, plus there's some risk of us getting to eighty dollars per unit in material cost. We still have a lot of work to do there."

"I hope you're right, Doug," said Kulig, sounding unconvinced. He turned to Porter again, "What do you think, Dave?"

Porter kept staring at the screen. "I don't know, it's just not how we've done things in the past," he said finally. It was clear this was against everything he believed in.

"Don't worry, Dave," I said. "These are just rough numbers, but we'll go through a more detailed analysis today and fine tune it so you feel more comfortable with it."

Porter, Evan, Alex, and I spent the next four hours going through the detailed P&L accounts allocating cost to the two business units using various drivers. First, we separated all material overhead-related costs such as warehousing, material handling, and material planners, which we then allocated based on actual inventory and inventory turns. Second, we assigned indirect labor to specific manufacturing lines. Third, we allocated salaried staff by effort using various measurable stats to determine effort. For example, the cost of the accounting staff was allocated using the number of invoices they had to write. Sure enough, about 70 percent of the invoices they had to process were appliance related, because of smaller volumes and higher mix of product. Electricity we allocated based on counters that each machine already had installed. There were only a few smaller items where we could not find a perfect driver to determine the split, but these were insignificant in the big scope of things, so we just made some rough guesses based on feedback from Rollins.

We also spent a couple of hours with Kulig and Rollins to determine what additional resources would be needed to run the Volta program. Fortunately, I was right there also, because most of the resources were already in place. We would obviously need to add two more shifts of direct laborers and the equivalent in indirect support staff, but everything else was pretty much in place. We would just need electricity to run the line #2 for two more shifts. Kulig also threw in a couple more people in the salaried staff to support launch, material planning, and accounting.

At the end of the exercise, the plant guys seemed to be on board with our calculations. Kulig brimmed with excitement and shook my hand so hard that I wanted to wince in pain.

"I think we're on to something, Doug," he said.

"Just make sure you tell the suits that," I joked. "I'll need all the support I can get to make people understand."

* * *

We said our goodbyes around 4:00 PM and drove out toward our next destination, the ECU housing supplier, three hours away. I looked over at my passengers, Evan and Alex. They looked pooped and just stared out of their respective windows.

"Well, it's time to reveal your answers," I announced and pulled two pieces of folded paper from my pocket.

"You can throw mine away," protested Evan from the front passenger seat.

I laughed. "I'm sure it's not so bad. Let's start with Alex."

Alex shifted uncomfortably in his seat. "I'd rather you didn't," he pleaded.

I unfolded his paper and read. "The problem is that the plant is not managing things properly, so the solution is to fire the plant manager and hire someone that knows what he's doing." I looked over at Evan, and we both burst out laughing. Alex looked uncomfortable at first, but then he laughed also. "Nice try, Alex," I finally said, "but before you start firing people, you might want to dig a little deeper into the problem."

"Sorry," he said, "these were very nice and smart people."

"Don't worry," I now tried to educate him, "sometimes we have to let people go, even when they are nice and smart, but it's always important to get a good diagnosis first. If you treat a skin rash not realizing that you have an allergy, then you'll probably treat it incorrectly."

Alex nodded in agreement.

"All right," I continued, "now it's Evan's turn." I opened the second piece of paper and read, "The problem is underutilization of the capacity and the solution is to increase utilization by adding programs to line #2." I looked over at Evan and smiled. "Very good. You basically got it. The question would be how to increase utilization, but you're correct."

"In my defense, I didn't know that marginal costing existed," said Evan. "I'm going to use that exclusively from now on."

"Well, it's not always appropriate, so you have to be careful," I warned him.

"What do you mean?" he replied, puzzled.

"Marginal costing on its own is of good use when you have an established plant and you're just adding to it. However, you have to be careful when you're quoting business that could drive significant additions to your current plant. A better way to think of it is by simply imagining the impact that any quoted business would make on your cost structure. And the best way to do that is to have a dynamic cost model, which predicts those impacts based on the various cost drivers that you establish. Think of it as levers and knobs on a furnace that you pull and adjust in order to control the heat and pressure inside the furnace. We're not going to have time to develop a model like that in just two weeks, but we'll do that after we're done with the Volta quote."

"Cool," is all that Evan had to say, but I could sense the satisfaction in his voice. He was excited to have a fresh new perspective. I remembered the first time I learned these concepts and how they opened my eyes. It was like finding out that the world is round and not flat. It took me away from the plug-and-chug mentality and gave me a big picture view of the costing world. I was hoping that Evan and Alex were going through the same realization.

Wednesday, Day 17 of 28

I felt exhausted when the alarm clock rang at 6 AM. The supplier of the ECU Housing, Tesung, insisted on taking us out to dinner the night before, and I could not say no to the purchasing manager, Carmen Lee, who thought it was necessary to maintain a good relationship with this Korean supplier. We had a great dinner at a local Korean restaurant, but I forgot how skilled Koreans are at drinking games. I stood no chance and again ended up drinking too much. My head now felt like a bowling ball awkwardly sitting on top of my neck and shoulders.

"Tesung are smart," said Lee who sat next to me as I drove to the supplier manufacturing plant. She insisted on driving with Evan, Alex, and I, while our cost estimators, Kumar, Navneeth, and Syed, together with the ECU Housing buyer, Jake Mullen, drove in a separate car. Lee was a petite woman, only in her early 30s, but she had the disposition of a high-ranking army general. She seemed completely unaffected by the alcohol she had consumed the night before, and she was now energetically typing away on her laptop as she spoke. "They owe me two million dollars this year for the Volta business, but have been delaying agreement because they know we have no other option but to go with them. This is a perfect opportunity to squeeze the money out of them."

I rubbed my eyes, trying to squeeze the hangover out of my head, took a large sip of my coffee, already a second cup this morning, then said, "You mean we are asking them to pay us two million up front for the business?"

"Yes, of course, that's our standard requirement. Plus, obviously, they have to give us three percent price reduction every year," she answered as if stating the obvious.

"How do you think they will come up with that money?"

"I don't understand. What do you mean?" she said, puzzled.

"I mean, it's a lot of money to come up with. Two million now, then, at a twenty dollar price and a million units per year, they have to give about six hundred thousand back every year," I said and was thankful that my brain was able to perform the calculation, "that's probably another four or five million dollars over program life that they have to give up."

"How did you get five million?" she protested. "It's only about six hundred thousand per year, so only about three million over five years that we book."

"That six hundred thousand reduction carries through every year for the supplier, so cumulatively speaking, they lose roughly five million in revenue, not just what you are able to book annually per Electronica's process."

"That's their problem, I guess," Lee announced. "I still want my money."

This was not helping my headache. Lee's words felt like a drill boring a hole in my brain. "Miss Lee, I apologize if I seem irritated, but it sounds like our new performance objectives were not communicated to you yet." She looked at me, confused, so I continued, "Your objective to get savings worth five percent of spend every year is no longer in place. Your main objective, from now on, is to contribute to profitable company growth."

"But this is what I'm good at," she said, almost pleading. "If I'm not here to get the annual savings, then what else am I supposed to do?"

"There are plenty of ways for you to contribute," I assured her. "For one, you can help me to negotiate a price down for the Volta housing. We have a six dollar gap to Navneeth's cost estimate."

She stared at me skeptically. "I have to call someone," she said finally as we pulled into Tesung's parking lot.

A whole congregation awaited us in a large modern conference room. There were at least 10 Korean men, all wearing the same blue frocks, and all greeting us with smiles and their business cards. Each of them bowed their head as they respectfully presented their business card with both hands, which is custom in many Asian countries. Between their group and ours, the process of exchanging business cards took at least 10 minutes.

"Thank you for having us," I announced as we settled in our chairs. "My name is Doug Benson and I'm the VP of Cost Engineering. You might be wondering why I am here and what is the objective of this visit?" I saw Tesung's whole team politely nod in unison, so I continued, "We are here because we need your help to win the Volta program. Our cost is not competitive and we need to find a way to reduce your housing price. Otherwise, neither Electronica nor Tesung will have this business." I took a moment to look around the room and let the message sink in.

"We have very good price for you," said one of the Tesung men with a heavy Korean accent who earlier introduced himself as Siyoung Park, their Director of Sales. He looked over at Carmen Lee and said, "We already agreed with Carmen."

I jumped in before Carmen could answer. "With all due respect, you can forget that agreement. That price will not work for us. We need to start from scratch."

A murmur went through the room. The Tesung team shifted in their chairs uncomfortably and whispered to each other in Korean. In the meantime, I grabbed the projector cable, connected it to my laptop, and projected a summary (see Table 3.6).

Table 3.6 ECU housing gap analysis

	Tesung	Target	Gap to target
Raw material	$3.76	$2.54	$1.23
Purchased components	$10.01	$7.67	$2.34
Labor	$0.60	$0.35	$0.25
Overhead	$1.64	$1.11	$0.52
Depreciation	$0.93	$0.54	$0.39
Scrap	$0.34	$0.24	$0.09
Freight and Duty	$0.85	$0.61	$0.24
Packaging	$0.17	$0.12	$0.05
Tooling	$0.47	$0.38	$0.09
SG&A	$1.02	$0.73	$0.28
Profit	$0.67	$0.49	$0.18
PRICE	$20.45	$14.78	$5.67

"We need the price to be at $14.78 in order to be competitive, which means we have over five and a half dollars to take out from your price," I said.

This statement elicited a chuckle from Park. "That's impossible," he said. "Your engineering would need to redesign."

"No," I stated firmly. "We need $14.78 for this design."

Park now seemed offended. "Your company always wants money from us. You say that you want three percent every year, but then you come and ask for five percent. Then, every time you give business, you want more money on top." He raised his arms and gave a death stare to Lee. "Where I find all this money?"

"I agree," I said and watched Park's face twist in confusion. "I want the best price up front and will not ask you to reduce that price for the rest of the program life. In fact, Electronica will never ask for price reductions or money up front unless we're giving you business that will improve your cost structure."

Park stared at me not knowing what to say. He looked over at Lee who was typing away on her laptop. "Is this true?" he finally spat out in disbelief.

"Yes, it's true," I assured him. "So, instead of pretending like your cost breakdown is real and wasting time trying to defend it, I would like you to take out any price reductions that you have built into your first year price and, after our team is done with a plant tour, come back with an updated cost breakdown that we can compare to our target. That will be the baseline of our discussion."

"That's not enough time, Mr. Benson," said another Tesung employee, Hajoon Chun, who was their quoting manager. "We have to get approval from Korea."

"I'm afraid we don't have more time," I said. "We need to finalize the agreement today. Call them right now and tell them to stay on standby until you have your bottom-line price finalized. Get an agreement from them prior to our discussion."

Park and Chun looked at each other skeptically. There was an awkward pause for a few seconds, then Park looked over at an older gentleman from Tesung's team that was sitting at the end of the table. This man gave me some nebulous title when he introduced himself to me earlier, but I assumed he was the most senior person in the room. He now nodded to Park in agreement.

"We agree," announced Park.

* * *

The plant tour was packed with at least 20 people between Tesung and Electronica employees. Like a dark cloud, we floated through the plant from one manufacturing process to another. Per the plant layout that we were given (see Figure 3.2), the raw materials in the form of copper coil and resin, arrived on the right side of the plant. The copper coil was stamped coil to coil and then sent out to a plating company. Upon return, the coils were again received and moved to the over molding presses. The resin was received mostly in a silo, from which the resin was distributed through overhead pipes to individual presses. However, a portion of the incoming warehouse was occupied by pallets of various resin in bags. These were for lower specialty volume applications. After the stampings were over molded with resin in one of the eight different molding cells, the finished housings were then moved to the outgoing warehouse.

What was interesting about the process was that the stamping and molding were two very different worlds. The stamping was very loud and dirty, and it required an operator on each press with a lot of effort to maintain production. Per our tour guide, who was the supervisor of this department, the machine uptime was about 65 percent across the four stamping presses. This was mostly due to the high number of tool and coil changeovers that took at least an hour each to perform. On the other side of the wall were the quiet and clean overmolding press cells that were basically operator-free. These were fully automated and performed cutting of pins from the coil, inserting them into a fixture, overmolding, inspection, electrical testing and packing into plastic trays. There were only two technicians per shift in the department, and they were mostly monitoring the machines. In fact, the human interaction was so minimal that the lights would only go on if the sensor detected movement outside the molding cells. Per the tour guide, the uptime in this department was almost 100 percent.

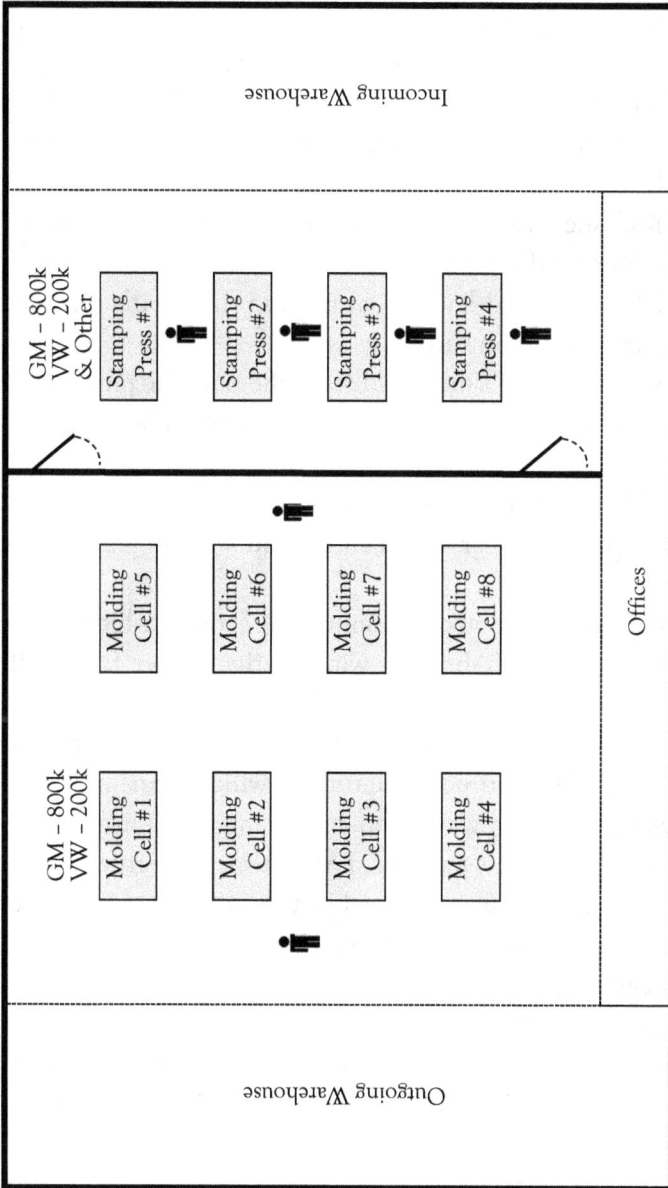

Figure 3.2 Tesung plant layout

The factory's equipment was fully utilized already, and Electronica's GM and VW programs were utilizing most of a stamping press and one complete molding cell. There was no open capacity for the Volta program being quoted, so Tesung was planning to outsource stamping to another company and squeeze another molding cell within the current floor plan.

"It looks like you're measuring cycle time," I said to Carmen Lee who stood by the molding cell staring at her Apple wrist watch.

"Yes," she answered and pressed the watch's tiny screen. "It's one minute and forty eight seconds."

"Oh!" I stepped back in surprise as this clearly was not the cycle time. "Are you sure?"

"Yes, of course. I measured from the time the pins are picked up by the robot arm until the time the finished housing is put in the packaging tray."

"If that was the cycle time, then they could never produce one million parts per year that the GM and VW programs require," I tried to explain.

"I think you're talking about TAKT time, which has to be eighteen seconds," she said with a grin on her face as if she caught a child miscalculating his fingers.

"Actually," I tried to correct her without sounding condescending, "TAKT time is the time in which a part must be produced in order to meet customer demand and it just so happens that the cycle time matches TAKT time at eighteen seconds. That means that a part is placed in a tray every eighteen seconds. What you calculated is the processing time, which is a time from the beginning to the end of the manufacturing process that a part goes through."

She stared at me for a few seconds then shook her head and said, "No, that's not right." After which she promptly walked away.

I was not going to chase her in order to convince her of what I said, but I was hoping to catch up with her later regarding this topic. I also took a mental note to develop some training for our purchasing team, and maybe engineering, to teach some manufacturing and costing principles. Tesung and other suppliers would not be impressed to know that our purchasing managers did not know what a cycle time was. More importantly, I did not want suppliers to take advantage of that weakness.

* * *

After returning to the conference room and eating lunch there, the discussion on pricing ensued, and it became heated quickly. Tesung had the new cost breakdown displayed (see Table 3.7) on the screen, and they were still far off from our target price.

"I appreciate you lowering the price to $18.05, but we still have over three dollars in gap to our target," I said. "How are you going to address the remaining three dollars?"

"That's the best we can do, Doug," said Park. "This is ten percent reduction and my boss in Korea was not happy."

I updated my gap analysis while he spoke and now projected it on the screen (see Table 3.8). "It looks like all you did was reduce your purchased component costs, which is mostly plating. Then, some other costs decreased because they were just percentages applied on top of manufacturing cost. Is that correct?"

"That's correct," replied Park without missing a beat. "I can be honest, we had to put the givebacks somewhere. But now, this is best price up front with your agreement that you will not ask for more money now or later. This price will stay for rest of the program. Correct?"

"If we agree on the price, then correct, it will stay for the rest of the program. But, I do not agree to this price," I stated. "And, I will tell you why. Number one, your copper scrap resale value assumes only 12.5% of the original cost, while copper scrap is currently selling at about 80% on the market today. That's about eighty cents in cost gap right there." Park said something in Korean to another gentlemen on their team, which I assumed to

Table 3.7 Updated ECU housing cost breakdown from Tesung

COST ESTIMATE – BREAKDOWN SHEET

Supplier Name:	Tesung
Program(s):	Volta
Part Number:	NA
Part Description:	ECU Housing
Additional Information:	NA
Prepared by:	Ben Kim

Date:	NA
RFQ Number	
ECN #:	NA

Yellow Cells are for Input
Blue Cells are for Output Results

Total Volume:	10,00,000
Supplier Mfg. Location:	USA
Supplier Shipping Location:	USA
Currency:	Dollar
Exchange Rate:	

A) RAW MATERIAL:

RAW MATERIAL COST

MATERIAL DESCRIPTION	Raw Material Stock Size (LxWxP/m)	Gross Material Weight	Net Material Weight	Unit of Measure	Cost/Unit
Copper coil		0.3400	0.1290	kg	$8.10
Resin		0.0200	0.4000	kg	$2.40
				TOTALS	

ENGINEERED SCRAP

Eng. Scrap Weight	Eng. Scrap Resale	Gross Raw Material Cost Total	Eng. Scrap Resale Cost/Unit	Eng. Scrap Credit (Ear)
0.2200	$2.7540		$1.0000	$0.2200
0.0800	$1.2000		$5.3600	$0.0135
		TOTALS		$0.2435

TOTAL

Total Raw Material Cost
$2.5340
$1.2375
$3.7666

COST PARETO CHART (% of total)

B) PURCHASED COMPONENTS & MATERIAL:

PURCHASED MATERIAL COSTS

ITEM DESCRIPTION	Supplier Name	Number of Unit(s)	Unit of Measure	Cost/Unit
Pin Plating		1		$1.0300
Blade Plating		1		$1.3000
Epoxy		1		$2.0000
Other		1		$1.5200

TOTAL

Purchased Materials
$1.0300
$1.3000
$2.0000
$1.5200
$3.9100

C) PROCESS COSTS:

PROCESS TIME PER PIECE

PROCESS DESCRIPTION	Part Cycle Time (sec)	Utilization(%)	Pieces Per Cycle	Standard hr/pc	Labour Standard hr/pc
Stamping Pin 1	1.0	60%	1	0.0002	0.0002
Stamping Pin 2	1.0	60%	1	0.0002	0.0002
Stamping Blade 1	1.0	60%	1	0.0002	0.0002
Stamping Blade 2	1.0	60%	1	0.0002	0.0002
Pre-assembly	40.0	90%	2	0.0060	0.0060
Overmolding	65.0	90%	2	0.0081	0.0081
Final Assembly	80.0	90%	2	0.0063	0.0063

DIRECT LABOR COST

Base Labour Rate ($/hr)	No. Of Operators	Labour Cost ($)
$30.00	1	$0.01
$30.00	1	$0.0050
$30.00	1	$0.0050
$30.00	1	$0.0050
$30.00	1	$0.1500
$30.00	1	$0.2438
$30.00	1	$0.1875
	TOTALS	$0.6013

OVERHEADS

Hourly Oil Rate ($/hr)	Oil Cost ($)
$30.00	$0.01
$30.00	$0.0050
$40.00	$0.0067
$40.00	$0.0067
$60.00	$0.3000
$100.00	$0.8125
$80.00	$0.5000
TOTALS	$1.6368

CAPITAL

Hourly Depreciation Rate ($/hr)	Depreciation Cost ($)	Total Labour & Oil Cost
$7.00	$0.00	$0.0112
$7.00	$0.0050	$0.0112
$15.60	$0.0025	$0.0142
$15.60	$0.0025	$0.0142
$31.50	$0.1550	$0.4600
$66.40	$0.4144	$1.4706
$66.00	$0.3500	$1.0375
TOTALS	$0.9267	$3.1628

D) LOGISTICS, PACKAGING & AMORTISATION:

Cost Type	Description		Cost / Piece
FREIGHT	Cost %	4.0%	0.5974
PACKAGING	Cost %	1.0%	0.1493
DUTY & WAREHOUSE	Cost %	1.0%	0.1493
TOOLING AMORTIZATION	Interest %	9.0%	1.1318
TOOLING BAR	Cost %	2.0%	0.2987
TOTALS			1.3266

TOTAL COST

MANUFACTURING COST (A+B+C)	$14.8342
FREIGHT, PACK, AMORTISATIONS	$1.3266
Scrap	2.0%
SG&A	6.0%
Profit %	4.0%

Scrap	$0.3091
SG&A	$0.6474

TARGET PRICE $18.0529

% of Total

RAW MATERIAL	20.9%
PURCHASED PARTS	44.4%
LABOR & OVERHEAD	17.5%
SCRAP	1.7%
AMORTISATION	6.3%
LOGISTICS & PACKAGING	5.0%
SG&A	5.0%
PROFIT	3.7%

Table 3.8 *Updated ECU housing gap analysis*

	Tesung	Tesung updated	Target	Gap to target	Gap to target updated
Raw material	$3.76	$3.76	$2.54	$1.23	$1.23
Purchased components	$10.01	$8.01	$7.67	$2.34	$0.34
Labor	$0.60	$0.60	$0.35	$0.25	$0.25
Overhead	$1.64	$1.64	$1.11	$0.52	$0.52
Depreciation	$0.93	$0.93	$0.54	$0.39	$0.39
Scrap	$0.34	$0.30	$0.24	$0.09	$0.05
Freight and Duty	$0.85	$0.75	$0.61	$0.24	$0.14
Packaging	$0.17	$0.15	$0.12	$0.05	$0.03
Tooling	$0.47	$0.43	$0.38	$0.09	$0.05
SG&A	$1.02	$0.90	$0.73	$0.28	$0.16
Profit	$0.67	$0.60	$0.49	$0.18	$0.11
Price	$20.45	$18.06	$14.78	$5.67	$3.28

be the purchasing manager. "Number two," I continued, "your plating, epoxy and other purchased component costs are still too high. I hope you're not simply hiding profit in those buckets, because I was hoping we would have an honest discussion."

I touched a nerve because Park almost jumped out of his chair with a protest. "We are not allowed to have profit above four percent and SG&A above six percent. This is your direction."

Now I was taken back. "What do you mean you're not allowed?" I asked.

"Your Purchasing says that we're not allowed to go over those percentages in the cost breakdown. Otherwise, they get in trouble explaining it in sourcing council."

We both looked over at Carmen Lee who simply stared at her laptop screen and did not say a word. It was obviously true.

"In that case," I said, "I will need you to forget that requirement. Your profit requirements are your business and I can't tell you what your profit should be. You should make as much profit as you want as long as your price is competitive."

Park was confused and kept looking at Lee for confirmation. When she did not give him any, he said, "So, you want us to update the cost breakdown again?"

"Yes," I said. "Put in whatever profit you are actually assuming. Same for SG&A, but keep in mind that this Volta business is a million units, so every dollar of SG&A is a million dollars per year that you'll be adding to your current SG&A cost. This might not make sense considering you already have people in place today being paid for by a fully utilized plant.

"Also, before you go back to update your cost breakdown, please also address your processing cost where we have over one dollar in gap. And, I see many issues. First, the cycle time for your molding should be 18 seconds per part, because your mold cycle time is 36 seconds for two cavities. Two, you only have a quarter of an operator assigned to that process today, not one operator like you indicated. Finally, your labor and overhead rates are higher than what we thought they should be. So, please make sure you are honest in your updated cost breakdown or we'll be here for a very long time."

Park stared at me for a moment, then looked over at the older gentleman at the end of the table who nodded in agreement. "Can we have one hour please?" asked Park.

* * *

One hour later, we gathered again and Park projected another cost breakdown on the screen (see Table 3.9). The price was now down to 16.27 U.S. dollars, even though the SG&A was at 15 percent and profit at 8 percent.

"This is our best and final offer," Park announced.

"Thank you," I said. "I appreciate you reducing your price and, more importantly, to provide an honest cost breakdown. This makes it much easier to have an honest discussion and easier to try and find cost reduction opportunities collaboratively."

"We cannot reduce cost any further. This is our best and final offer," reiterated Park.

Table 3.9 *Updated ECU housing cost breakdown from Tesung*

COST ESTIMATE - BREAKDOWN SHEET

Supplier Name:	Tesung
Program(s):	Volts
Part Number:	NA
Part Description:	ECU Housing
Additional Information:	NA
Prepared by:	Ben Kim

Date:	
RFQ Number	NA
ECN #:	NA

Total Volume:	10,00,000
Supplier Mfg. Location:	USA
Supplier Shipping Location:	USA
Currency:	Dollar
Exchange Rate:	

Yellow Cells are for Input
Blue Cells are for Output Results

A) RAW MATERIAL:

RAW MATERIAL COST

MATERIAL DESCRIPTION	Raw Material Stock Size (LxWxTH)	Gross Material Weight	Net Material Weight	Unit of Measure	Cost/Unit
Copper coil		0.3490	0.1200	kg	$6.16
Resin		0.5000	0.4600	kg	$2.98
				TOTAL 9	

ENGINEERED SCRAP

Eng. Scrap Weight	Eng. Scrap Resale Cost/Unit	Eng. Scrap Resale Cost/Total	Eng. Scrap Credit (Eur)
0.2290	$6.5460		$1.4395
0.0400	$0.3560		$1.1376
TOTALS			$1.4913

TOTAL

Gross Raw Material Cost Total	Total Raw Material Cost
$2.7540	$1.3162
$1.3600	$1.2376
TOTALS	
$4.0040	$2.6627

B) PURCHASED COMPONENTS & MATERIAL:

PURCHASED MATERIAL COSTS

ITEM DESCRIPTION	Supplier Name	Number of Unit(s)	Unit of Measure	Cost/Unit
Pin Plating		1		$0.8500
Blade Plating		1		$1.2900
Epoxy		1		$2.2960
Other		1		$3.5260

TOTAL

Purchased Materials
$0.8500
$1.2900
$2.2960
$3.5260
TOTALS $7.7200

C) PROCESS COSTS:

PROCESS TIME PER PIECE

PROCESS DESCRIPTION	Pure Cycle Time (sec)	Utilization(%)	Pieces Per Cycle	Standard In/pc	Labor Standard hr/pc
Stamping Pin 1	1.0	60%	1	0.0002	0.0002
Stamping Pin 2	1.0	60%	1	0.0002	0.0002
Stamping Blade 1	1.0	60%	1	0.0002	0.0002
Stamping Blade 2	1.0	60%	2	0.0002	0.0002
Pre-Assembly	36.0	90%	2	0.0045	0.0011
Overmolding	36.0	90%	2	0.0045	0.0011
Final Assembly	36.0	90%	2	0.0045	0.0011

DIRECT LABOR COST

No. Of Operators	Base Labour Rate ($/hr)	Labour Cost ($)
1	$30.00	$0.61
1	$30.00	$0.0050
1	$30.00	$0.0050
1	$30.00	$0.0050
0.25	$30.00	$0.0338
0.25	$30.00	$0.0338
0.25	$30.00	$0.0338
TOTALS		$0.1213

OVERHEADS

Hourly OH Rate ($/hr)	OH Cost ($)
$30.00	$0.0067
$30.00	$0.0050
$40.00	$0.0067
$40.00	$0.0067
$40.00	$0.2700
$100.00	$0.0800
$80.00	$0.3600
TOTALS	$1.1633

CAPITAL

Hourly Depreciation Rate ($/hr)	Depreciation Cost ($)
$7.00	$0.60
$7.00	$0.0012
$15.00	$0.0025
$18.00	$0.0025
$33.00	$0.1355
$84.00	$0.2295
$56.00	$0.2520
TOTALS	$6.6293

TOTAL COST

Total Labour & OH Cost
$0.0172
$0.0112
$0.0142
$0.0142
$0.4413
$0.7133
$0.6458
$1.9325

D) LOGISTICS, PACKAGING & AMORTISATION:

Cost Type	Description	Cost / Piece
FREIGHT	Cost % 4.0%	0.4864
PACKAGING	Cost % 1.0%	0.1216
DUTY & WAREHOUSE	Cost % 1.0%	0.1216
TOOLING AMORTIZATION	Interest % 9.0%	0.1316
TOOLING S&A	Cost % 2.0%	0.2427
TOTALS		1.1036

TOTAL COST

MANUFACTURING COST (A+B+C)	$13.1366
FREIGHT, PACK, AMORTISATIONS	$1.1036
Scrap 2.0%	$0.3427
SG&A 10.0%	$1.9253
Profit % 8.0%	$0.6708
TARGET PRICE	**$16.2721**

% of Total

RAW MATERIAL	16.7%
PURCHASED PARTS	47.5%
LABOR & OVERHEAD	11.4%
SCRAP	3.8%
AMORTIZATION	0.8%
LOGISTICS & PACKAGING	4.0%
SG&A	11.2%
PROFIT	6.0%

COST PARETO CHART (% of total)

"I understand and I'm ok with most of it, but your overhead rates are still high, both manufacturing overhead and corporate overhead, or SG&A. Maybe you can educate me, what goes into your SG&A cost?"

Park squirmed in his chair uncomfortably. He was obviously hoping that the conversation would be over, and he did not want to open things up for further negotiation. "We have a lot of cost," he finally spoke up. "We have sales, finance, accounting, HR, IT and all of their offices and equipment and travel. But, on top of that, we have to pay for R&D somehow, which is not separated in your cost breakdown form. You pay us for ED&T, which is application engineering cost, but we also have people who are developing and researching new products and technology, so we have to pay for that somehow. Then, we have startup costs at the beginning of the program that we need to amortize. And, of course, we have risk that we need to account for in case something goes wrong. So, there is a lot of cost in SG&A."

"That makes sense," I confirmed. "And how much of that 15% SG&A cost is risk?"

"Five percent," said Park cautiously.

"That's the only one that I don't agree with," I stated and watched Park sit up in alarm. "Five percent is equivalent to about sixty cents or six hundred thousand per year that I would be paying you in oops money. So, if nothing goes wrong, that money turns into profit for you. If something does go wrong, let's say you have a quality spill, then I will ask you to pay me back for damages and you'll just use the money I already paid you to now pay me. Does that sound like something I, as a customer, would want to pay for?"

Park looked puzzled and could not find words to explain it. I figured he probably never even thought about that five percent and just took it for what it was. Most likely, nobody ever challenged him on it.

"Mister Benson," said the elder Korean gentleman at the end of the table. His voice was much deeper than I expected, and it seemed to startle everyone in the room to attention. "We don't have the approval from Korea to change that, but I understand your point. However, you must understand that we might not be able to execute to our best assumptions up front, so we need some wiggle room in case we cannot perform at the cycle time or the capacity utilization that we assumed."

His excellent English surprised me, and it took me a second to respond. "I understand where you're coming from, but you are currently making very similar products at the assumed cycle time and utilization. You must understand that I would not want to pay you in case you screw it up. I would be giving you an incentive not to try hard to be perfect."

The elderly man nodded and said, "I understand. I will discuss with my Korean colleagues and have an answer to you tomorrow."

"Thank you. I appreciate your cooperation," I replied. "However, I would like you to address one more problem with your piece cost. Your manufacturing overhead rates are a bit too high also. I assume you're using current budget rates for your assumption, which is based on the plant's full utilization. However, by squeezing another molding cell in here, you're actually taking the plant utilization above 100% and will be improving the fixed cost absorption, which means that your overhead rates should actually decrease. So, I would like you to also consider reducing your manufacturing burden rates."

The older man nodded again and waved at Park to continue.

"We will get back to you tomorrow, Doug," said Park.

"Two more things we need to discuss," I announced to Park's horror. Even the older man seemed to be alarmed. "First, I'd like to hear your ideas on how we can change the design or manufacturing process to reduce cost further."

Park seemed to breathe a sigh of relief as we moved off commercial issues. "We actually provided some ideas to your engineering team but they decided against those," he said.

"Please share with me," I insisted. "I will take it back and evaluate again."

"Well, we think that the pin shape is too complex and causes a lot of scrapped copper. We can resell scrap at 65% of original value here locally, but reducing scrap would still help reduce cost."

I wrote as he spoke. "Yes, that's perfect. What else?"

"The plating seems excessive also. You use gold on all your pins, but your competition mostly uses silver. Your competition uses a lot more compliant pins as well, so pre-made pins that are just pressed into the housing instead of making custom pins that have to be over-molded into the housing. Also, your resin grade is much higher than your competition and very expensive. Finally, for some reason, your specification requires us to do the electrical test twice. Nobody else does that and we never had any rejects on the second test, so we're not sure why it's needed."

"Very good," I said after I finished writing it all down. "This is exactly what we're looking for." Park breathed a sigh of relief, but I continued. "How much are these cost reduction ideas worth?"

"I will send you the proposal we sent to Engineering," Park reassured me. "But, it's worth about fifty cents."

"Navneeth," I said and looked over at our cost estimator, "what do you think these changes are worth?"

Navneeth seemed shocked that anyone would address him, but he sat up in his chair and put on a brave face. "I would have to run a calculation, but probably around two dollars," he said.

"That sounds about right," I agreed. "I'm willing to share the savings 50/50, but nothing more and nothing less. We both need good motivation to make these happen."

Park looked over at his team and got no disagreements, so he nodded his head. "We agree," he said. "You mentioned there's another thing?" asked Park with apprehension.

"Yes," I said. "We also need to address your tooling cost. It's over two hundred thirty thousand higher than what we estimated."

Park's elbows fell on the table with desperation. He looked at his watch and said, "It's getting kind of late, is this something we can discuss another time?"

"Unfortunately, no," I stated firmly. "We don't have any more time. Our quote to Volta is due next week. This needs to be resolved today."

We spent the next hour going through the details of the tooling quote, which consisted of multiple stamping and molding tools as well as various assembly fixtures. Based on the discussion, it was obvious that the tooling was a profit generator for them as well. Even though they purchased tools from other suppliers, they threw a markup on top of it to make money. They also treated tooling cost as pass-through cost to us, so they did not spend much time challenging their tooling suppliers, and all the cost assumptions were very robust, meaning that they were hiding a lot of profit. After much negotiation, Tesung finally agreed to reduce their tooling bill by 150,000 U.S. dollars, even though they claimed not to have the authority to do so.

Thursday, Day 18 of 28

Another day, another supplier. This time we were off to visit Concordia, a manufacturer of aluminum blocks. Concordia has been around for 50 years, and I was told by Carmen Lee that they might not be around for much longer. Somehow this company managed to continue to lose business year after year, and Electronica was one of their few remaining customers. They declined to invite us out to dinner the night before, politely suggesting that they could not afford such extravagance. I decided not to insist or pay for it ourselves because I needed time to rest and catch up on my sleep.

Concordia's plant manager, Matt Anderson, a short stocky man in his 50s, and his team gave us a friendly welcome, but I got a sense of gloom behind the forced smiles and their unkempt building confirmed it. The grass outside has not been mowed in weeks, the paint has not been refreshed in years, the office furniture was old and falling apart, and the floors were not swept or mopped. Perhaps, the situation here was even worse than what Lee described. If this supplier was in such financial situation that they could not even spend money on upkeep, then they might be close to bankruptcy, and our current production programs might be in jeopardy.

"Thank you for coming," stated Anderson, more out of mere courtesy than any real appreciation, as we settled in a conference room. "I hope that we can help you today."

"I am confident that we will be able to help each other," I countered trying to set the tone for our negotiation. "Maybe you can tell us more about the operations?"

"Of course," said Anderson and spread a large printout of the plant layout on the table (see Figure 3.3). "It's a pretty straight forward factory. We have thirty CNC machines, all exactly the same, and a washing line that we run the parts through after machining," he explained as I looked over the layout. "That's pretty much it."

I nodded my head in agreement. "And you have all these operators? One per CNC?" I asked.

"Well, not exactly," he admitted. "We would if we were running all the machines, but we're only at about fifty percent utilization right now."

That was a red flag. At 50 percent utilization, it was unlikely that this machine shop was making any money.

Anderson saw the concern on my face, so he continued, "Between those thirty machining centers, we have about 180,000 of available machining hours. That assumes 120 hours per week with three shifts per day. But, we are only able to run two shifts per day and only some of the machines, so our actual hours of operation are only about 90,000."

"That's not good," I stated the obvious with sincere concern. "What happened to the other fifty percent of utilization? Why aren't you able to fill it?"

Anderson sighed in frustration. "I've been here for twenty years and honestly I couldn't tell you for sure. We lost a large chunk of business to another customer about ten years ago and we have not been competitive ever since. We've lost a lot

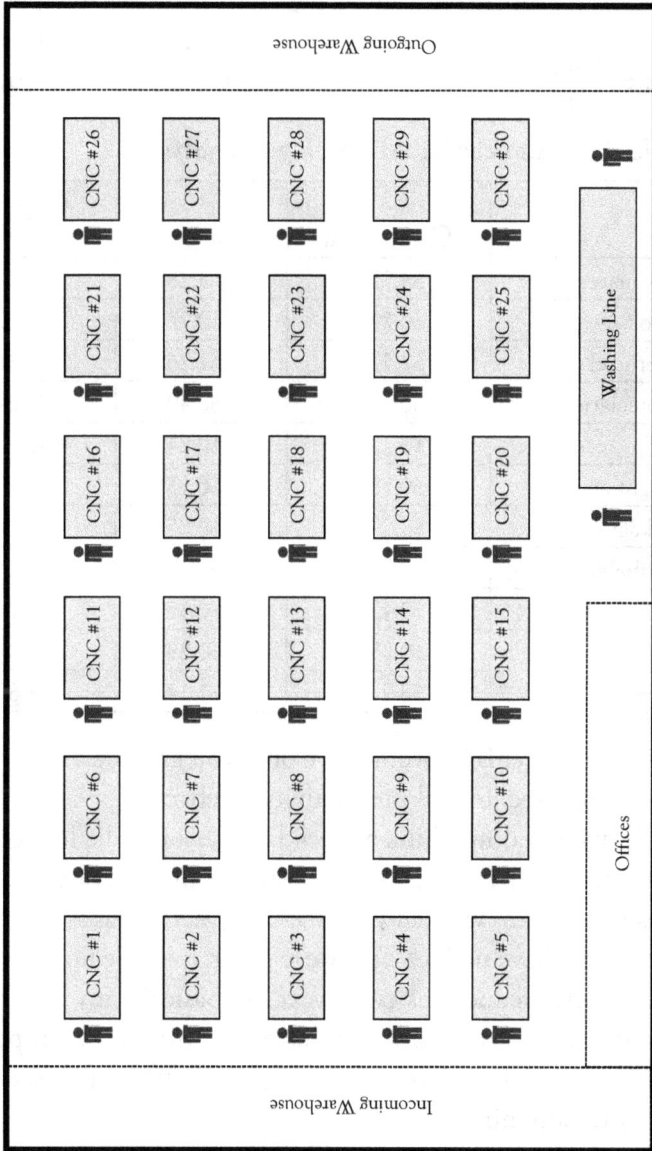

Figure 3.3 Concordia plant layout

of business to Chinese and Korean competitors, but this is not a labor intensive process and the freight to bring it over here would offset any labor. Plus, at full utilization, I can probably reduce the labor even more by having one operator run two CNCs at the same time. So, I really don't know what happened."

"I appreciate your candidness," I said and projected my screen on the wall (see Table 3.10). "From what I can tell, most of your

Table 3.10 *Concordia AL block gap analysis*

	Concordia	Target	Gap to target
Raw material	$3.52	$3.28	$0.24
Labor	$0.79	$0.72	$0.07
Overhead	$2.57	$1.26	$1.31
Depreciation	$0.53	$0.49	$0.04
Scrap	$0.22	$0.24	($0.02)
Freight and duty	$0.18	$0.15	$0.03
Packaging	$0.09	$0.05	$0.04
Perishable tooling	$0.35	$0.31	$0.04
SG&A	$0.45	$0.35	$0.10
Profit	$0.25	$0.29	($0.04)
Price	$8.96	$7.14	$1.82

gap to our target is in overhead. Could you give me a lower price if we eliminated annual productivity givebacks?"

"Actually, I don't think so," said Anderson as he looked over at one of the guys on his team. "Russell, our controller that prepares the quotes, will tell you that our price is based on today's cost and we have no idea how we're going to come up with three percent price reductions every year. It's basically my task to figure that out. Most likely, we'll have to continue to cut people, that's the only cost lever that I have left. We're not spending money on anything else."

I looked over at my team and saw that they were looking at me for answers. I think we were all feeling sincere sympathy for this company, probably because Electronica has been going through the same type of difficulties as Concordia.

"Let me ask you, Russell," I said, "How do you calculate your overhead cost?"

Russell, also a stocky short man, but maybe in his early 40s, stirred in his chair, uncomfortable with the spotlight landing on him. "Like we've always done it," he said defensively. "We have our cost defined per standard hour and then we multiply that by the cycle time."

"And how is your cost per standard hour calculated?" I pushed further.

"It's just our total overhead cost divided by total standard hours, which is about 90,000 per year like Matt said," replied Russell.

"Do you mean total overhead and total number of operating hours per last year results?" I asked.

"Yes, that's correct," both Russell and Matt answered at the same time.

"And this is how you've always calculated hourly overhead cost?"

They both nodded their heads in agreement, so I continued. "So, ever since you lost that big chunk of business ten years ago, your denominator in that equation, which is operating hours, has been decreasing. You've been cutting people to keep up, but your fixed costs probably can't be cut that much, since you still have a building and machines and salaried staff to pay for. So, your numerator has been decreasing, but at a much slower pace than your denominator. Therefore, every year, your overhead hourly rates keep going up and you keep quoting higher and higher overhead costs. And, every year, you become less and less competitive. Is that correct?"

Anderson and Russell looked at each other. "Yes, I guess," Anderson agreed.

"And how do you suppose you can get out of that death spiral?" I asked.

They shrugged their shoulders still unclear of how to help themselves.

"You'll never win business if you don't quote to your optimal capacity utilization," threw out Evan who was sitting next to me. He looked at me for confirmation, and I nodded my head in agreement while beaming with pride seeing young Evan figuring things out, so he continued, "You're basically asking customers to pay for your open capacity, to pay you for your machines sitting idle half the time. And obviously, your customers have rejected that deal. So, the only way to climb out of that hole is to quote all future business under the assumption that your plant will be fully utilized."

"This will result in lower prices," I stated confidently. "You can cut about a dollar out of your price if you did that. That will be very attractive to a lot of customers, including Electronica. And I will not ask you for any price reductions over the program life."

Anderson looked at Evan and me for a moment, then said, "Can Russell and I have a moment?"

It took two more hours of discussion and helping them develop a bit more detailed model of their cost structure under full utilization, but ultimately they agreed to reduce their price while also giving us some ideas to reduce cost through design modifications. I insisted that they use their new cost model for all their customers going forward; otherwise, they would not be able to fill out that open capacity. They agreed to do that and also made plans to improve operator utilization as more machines were utilized.

Friday, Day 19 of 28

After spending four nights in four different hotels, I woke up completely disoriented. I got confused about what side of the bed I am supposed to get up at and stubbed my toe on a chair. While wincing in pain, I then tried to get into the bathroom using the wrong door and then could not locate the toilet once inside the bathroom. Thank goodness that today was the last day of our trip.

Our last supplier to visit was Kymex, a manufacturer of connectors and wire harnesses, and this negotiation was not going to be easy. Considering that Kymex was actually a bigger company than Electronica and not very cooperative historically, per Carmen Lee, we had a big challenge in front of us trying to lower their price. It would have been nice to meet with their staff for dinner the night before, but they were not available, which told me that our business was not that important to them.

"Are you ready?" I asked Evan as we pulled up into Kymex's parking lot. I requested that he lead the negotiation today and saw that he was nervous.

"We'll find out soon," he said cryptically.

"Don't worry, I'll be there to back you up," I assured him.

We were greeted by Mike Sullivan, Kymex's sales director. He was a younger man, very handsome and athletic, and very natural with pleasantries. However, as we arrived to an empty conference room, I began to worry that these guys were not taking us seriously. We were obviously not a priority for them if they did not bother to show up on time or to greet us as a team.

"I apologize, but our plant manager and controller got hung up with something else and won't join us for another half hour," said Sullivan as we settled in. "But, in the meantime, I can show you the volume trend and why we're asking for price increases on your parts."

Evan looked at me and I looked over at Carmen who did not tell us anything about price increases.

"Sorry, Mike," said Carmen. "As I told you before, we will not entertain any price increases on current production parts. We're here to talk about the Volta program only and the pricing we need in order to win that business."

"Before we get into any pricing discussions," I interrupted, "perhaps we can take a tour of the facility? I don't want to waste this time talking about pricing without even understanding your manufacturing operations."

Sullivan did not seem thrilled about my suggestion. "The tour was scheduled for this afternoon…"

"And our meeting was scheduled for ten minutes ago," I cut him off.

"Let me see what I can do," he conceded and got on his phone.

Twenty minutes later, we were on the manufacturing floor being led by one of Kymex's manufacturing engineers, Art Angelakis. The factory was a large well-run facility, and the production was vertically integrated with stamping, plating, molding, overmolding, and assembly operations all in-house (see Figure 3.4). Art explained to us that the plant was fully utilized, and that they were considering expansion in order to accommodate our Volta program. The efficiency was also very good, at around 90 percent, and they had their changeovers down to half an hour, even on stamping presses.

I noticed Evan taking more of a leadership role during the tour. He asked a lot of questions about the manufacturing operations and also engaged Carmen and our cost estimators discussing various aspects of it. At one point, I saw him compare notes with Carmen and Navneeth on cycle time measurement for the molding process.

Kymex's general manager, Jon Steward, and controller, Libin Michael, were already waiting for us when we got back to the conference room. Steward was an energetic gray-haired 60-something-year-old, while Michael was an Indian man in his 40s who had an Ivy League aura about him.

"Thank you for having us," Evan jumped right in. "This is a great facility. Very well run." The Kymex team nodded their head in appreciation. "However, we have a big issue. Our cost estimator, Navneeth, has developed an estimate for the Volta header and it is forty percent lower than your quoted price."

Sullivan chuckled dismissively. "C'mon, that can't be right," he spat out.

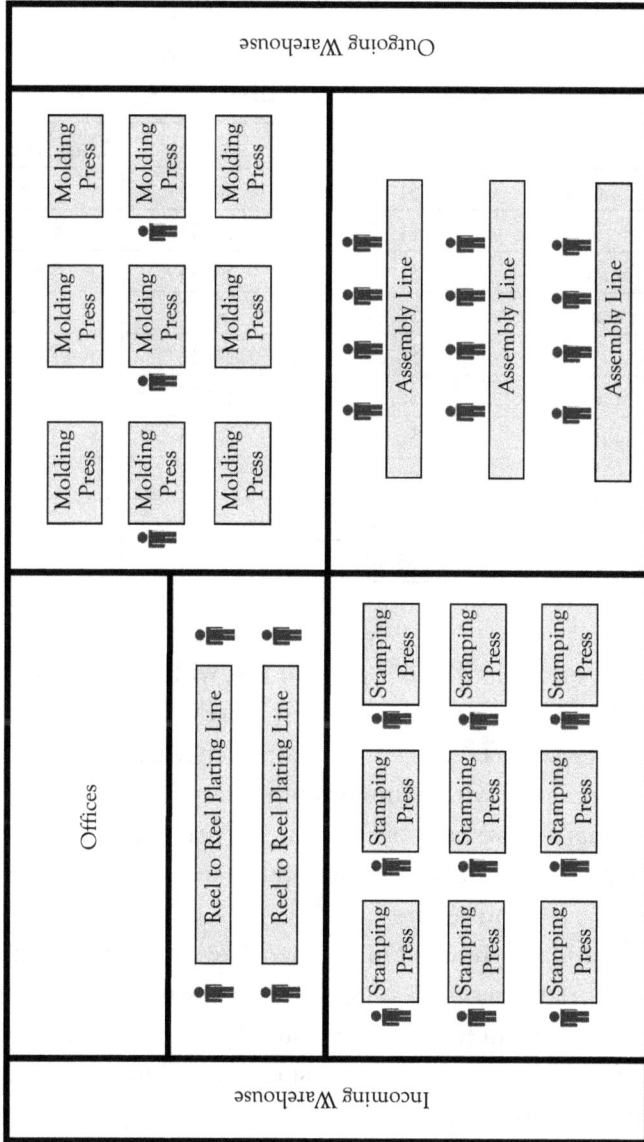

Figure 3.4 Kymex plant layout

"Actually, that's what I thought also," said Evan and projected a cost breakdown comparison (see Table 3.11). "However, we verified during the plant tour that all of his assumptions were correct. Machine sizes, manning, cycle times, it all checks out."

Table 3.11 Kymex header gap analysis

	Kymex	Target	Gap to target
Raw material	$1.34	$0.45	$0.89
Labor	$1.23	$0.52	$0.71
Overhead	$1.97	$1.34	$0.63
Depreciation	$0.49	$0.41	$0.08
Scrap	$0.20	$0.21	($0.01)
Freight and duty	$0.15	$0.15	$0.00
Packaging	$0.09	$0.05	$0.04
SG&A	$0.30	$0.17	$0.13
Profit	$0.20	$0.15	$0.05
Price	$5.98	$3.45	$2.53

"Isn't our Volta Header price in line with what you're paying today for current production parts?" pitched in Steward.

"That's correct," agreed his controller Michael. "We quoted you consistently with your current pricing."

"Perhaps we've been overpaying for years," stated Evan flatly.

"Wait a second," interrupted Sullivan. "We bid these competitively, fair and square."

"Yes and no," jumped in Carmen. "Yes, we gave you the business, but our customers suggested we go with you even though we had lower prices from other suppliers. One of the suppliers was actually very close to our cost estimate, but we dismissed it, just like the estimate."

"Not to be rude," said Sullivan, "but why don't you just go with that supplier then?"

Carmen looked over at me and Evan as if looking for permission to say something. Sullivan was throwing out a challenge, calling our bluff on competitive leverage, and I was not sure if anything that Carmen said was true.

"We might," stated Carmen with a poker face. "And I will take your current business with it. The Header design belongs to us, there is nothing preventing us from changing suppliers."

"Hold on," said Steward throwing his hands up, "let's not get crazy here. We appreciate your business and would love to grow with you."

This was a good sign. The general manager jumping in meant that he was making good money off of our parts and wanted to maintain it in his business portfolio.

"How about this," I said, "you get to keep your current business and maintain those high margins, but give us the price we need on the Volta program? Keep in mind that we're talking about additional million parts per year and even with lower margins, that's still a lot of cash contributing toward profitability of your plant. And, if we don't get the price we need from you, then we don't win the business and you don't get any of that cash."

Sullivan shook his head in frustration, but Steward and Michael looked at each other as if a deal might be possible.

"Can you give us some time to think about this?" Steward asked.

"We need an answer today unfortunately," I replied. "We need some time to work with our plan B supplier if you don't agree to our proposal."

"I understand," said Steward. "We'll have an answer to you before you fly out."

Thus concluded our visit at Kymex. It was time to take off for the airport.

* * *

The supplier visits were finally completed and Evan, Alex, and I sat exhausted at one of the Charlotte airport restaurants. The rest of our team already took off on an earlier flight. My brain was fried, but I could not resist torturing my co-travelers with more cost engineering conversation.

"So, Alex," I said, "could you please summarize our negotiation with Concordia, our aluminum block supplier?"

Alex looked at me with tired contempt. "Of course," he said, but clearly meant to say something unkind. "It was all about their cost allocation method with fifty percent capacity utilization, which basically assumed that we were paying for all their open capacity. Then, we got some good ideas on reducing the cycle time by reducing our surface finish requirements, which are probably an over kill."

"Very good, Alex. And what was the solution to their quoting problem?"

"To quote based on a cost model that assumed a fully utilized plant at 120 hours per week and their normal uptime," said Alex.

"Correct. The only way to bring business back was to assume that you've already won that business and that your fixed cost was already fully absorbed. Although that will not fix their problems today, their prices will be competitive again and they will fill that plant again. If they don't do that, their prices will continue to be uncompetitive and their death spiral will continue until the factory has to close its doors."

"It seems kind of simple and obvious," said Alex. "Why couldn't they figure that out on their own?"

"Great question," I concurred. "Why wasn't Concordia, or Electronica for that matter, able to figure out their costing issues?"

"They didn't know a better method," said Evan. "They kept doing things the way they've always done them and assumed that was the only way to look at it. Concordia was using fully absorbed standard costs and Electronica was allocating overhead cost based on labor cost, which might have worked at some point, mostly for accounting purposes, but failed completely when trying to predict the future."

"Exactly," I said nodding my head eagerly in agreement. "What a lot of companies are missing is a dynamic cost model that can predict the future cost structure based on the business that is being quoted or the capacity utilization that a company wants to achieve."

"How about today's connector supplier, Kymex?" I continued. "Evan, you want to give us a summary?"

I gave Evan the lead on negotiations with Kymex, and he did an outstanding job. Kymex's factory was actually very well utilized, and they seemed to know how to cost their products. They were simply charging us at a price that has not been seriously challenged since three product generations ago, which was probably 10 years ago. It seemed that Electronica was perfectly happy with taking their standard price reductions annually, but nothing else.

"It was awesome," he said with a grin. "I can't believe they reduced their price by forty percent. We never challenged their price point, just kept assuming the same level of pricing for years. Thank goodness we had good estimates from Navneeth to challenge them with."

"That's exactly why you need cost estimating," I confirmed. "Without it, you might be under the assumption that getting a couple of percentage points off the price is a great deal, all the while you were off the target by forty percent. Just like a navigator needs navigation tools, a cost engineer needs good cost estimates to be successful."

"I don't think we made friends with Carmen Lee, though," said Evan. "You completely turned her world upside down."

"That's ok," I said with a smirk. I did not want to tell the guys, but Carmen actually apologized to me when she caught me alone at a hotel bar the night before. She admitted that she was wrong about the cycle time calculation, but went much further than that by telling me that she really loved my data-driven approach to the negotiation. She said that it opened her eyes to a completely new way of thinking, and she was now a believer in this method. "I'm hopeful she'll be able to learn from this experience and become a better buyer," is all I said to Evan and Alex who nodded their heads in agreement.

"Any common themes among the plants that we visited?" I asked them.

"Capacity!" shouted Evan like a student from the back of a packed university auditorium. He checked himself, then said,

"Sorry, I didn't mean to get excited. It just seems so obvious. You need to cost your products to specific capacity utilization that is achievable, yet so many people just use whatever capacity assumption is in place now or in the past."

I was proud to see Evan excited about his job again. "That's exactly right," I said. "Capacity utilization is the most important consideration when developing a model of your company's cost structure. You can have all the other things right, like cost allocation method or accuracy, but if you're doing it all with the wrong capacity utilization, then it will all be for naught."

Both Evan and Alex nodded their head in agreement. Evan opened his laptop and turned it toward me displaying an updated gap analysis for the Volta brake system (see Table 3.12).

Table 3.12 Updated BOM cost gap analysis

	Piece price	Target price	Gap	% Gap	Tooling	Target tooling	Gap	% Gap
ECU housing	$15.66	$14.78	$0.88	6%	$837,000	$750,000	$87,000	10%
AL block	$7.95	$7.14	$0.81	10%	$-	$-	$-	0%
PCB	$6.78	$6.25	$0.53	8%	$-	$-	$-	0%
Connector	$3.56	$3.45	$0.11	3%	$205,000	$175,000	$30,000	15%
Capacitors (large)	$5.72	$5.25	$0.47	8%	$-	$-	$-	0%
Micro	$3.50	$2.75	$0.75	21%	$-	$-	$-	0%
ICs	$3.45	$2.69	$0.76	22%	$-	$-	$-	0%
Other (electronic)	$15.67	$12.15	$3.52	22%	$-	$-	$-	0%
Other (mechanical)	$19.99	$14.27	$5.72	29%	$345,000	$250,000	$95,000	28%
TOTAL	$82.28	$68.73	$13.55	16%	$1,387,000	$1,175,000	$212,000	15%

"What you got there?" I asked him.

"If my calculation is right," said Evan, "then we got the BOM cost from $90 down to $82 level. I think you said we had to be around $80 in order to be profitable with $100 price to Volta, so we're almost there."

Alex and I both studied the summary, and it appeared that Evan was correct. We also reduced the tooling bill by another 184,000 U.S. dollars, which would improve our offer to Volta.

"Unfortunately, we won't have time to work with the other suppliers," I said. "So, maybe we can run the business case with two separate material line items, one line item with those three components without future piece price reductions and another line item with the rest of the BOM cost and our regular three percent annual discount. It will be interesting to see what profitability that results in."

"I can do that no problem," said Evan. "I can have something to you on Monday."

"Can't we just tell purchasing to make the same deal with other suppliers so that we don't have to assume annual price reductions for any of them?" asked Alex.

"Good point," I replied. "However, I would be cautious with all the electronic component suppliers. Their pricing is heavily based on price volume curves and they are used to building in price reductions for all their customers."

"What's a price volume curve?" asked Evan.

"This is where the price is dependent on the volume of parts that you're buying. So, if you buy one million microchips, the price is X, but if you buy five million, the price then could be X minus 30%. It doesn't matter what the actual cost is to make the part."

"So there's no way to negotiate based on cost just like we did with other suppliers?" asked Alex, surprised.

"It should be done that way and it's definitely possible, because electronic components are not magical and are manufactured in factories just like any other component," I said. "However, the electronic component industry has resisted this aggressively. Probably because they are afraid to lose their fat profit margins. At least, that's the perception."

The sandwiches that we ordered earlier finally arrived, so we broke up the discussion. Evan excused himself to go to the bathroom, and I was left alone with Alex. I realized this was the first time this whole trip that we were alone. As he always did during meals, he stared at his food as if he was afraid it would run away and avoided eye contact with me or anyone else.

"So, do you want to have a career in cost engineering?" I asked him.

It first looked like he wanted to agree with me, but then decided to be honest. "I'm not sure," he said. "I still have to finish college and I still have a lot to learn."

"Thank you for being honest with me. It sounds like there's something that you don't like about cost engineering?"

He chewed for a few seconds while staring at his sandwich then said, "It just seems like nobody really respects cost engineering. Before you joined us, it was kind of ignored and even now people are upset that you're telling them what to do.

"Plus, it doesn't seem like a good career move. Even though you learn so much in cost engineering, everything from design to manufacturing and finance, I have not seen Evan given any opportunities to advance. It seems like a dead end job."

I was now shocked by Alex's openness. This is the most he spoke since I met him and definitely the most insightful into his personality. "I agree with you," I said. "We will change that at Electronica, but I agree that this is usually the case. I could not tell you why that is or how we got to this point, but it's not like that in every country or every company. Regardless, we will turn cost engineering into a career path that is CEO worthy."

Alex nodded his head, but looked skeptical. "I'll probably go into design engineering," he stated and almost made me laugh. It was only because Evan returned that I did not laugh. Alex's response was funny, but his skepticism was not, and I knew it would be a long road to respectability for cost engineering. Even if we won the Volta business, there were just so many competing functions and priorities that respect was not guaranteed. I would have to work very hard to institutionalize cost engineering into our product and employee development processes.

CHAPTER 4

The Fix

Monday, Day 22 of 28

I woke up on Monday already stressed out. The fact that we only had five days to submit our new quote finally hit me, and I suddenly felt like a drowning person that is trying to come up for air. I was able to suppress the panic with my morning routine, but it returned as soon as I pulled up in front of Electronica's office building at 9:00 AM. I tried to think about Emily and the thought of being able to see her again took the edge off. We spoke on the phone over the weekend, which went well, but I was looking forward to seeing her in person again.

As soon as I entered the lobby, I knew something was off. The receptionist did not even look at me, and a man carrying a cardboard box full of office decorations passed me on his way out. As I walked up the stairs to get to my office, a young lady carrying a similar box passed me on her way down. I have seen this scene before, during the last recession, but I thought it impossible to happen here and now.

I rushed toward my office, but stopped cold seeing Stephanie, the hotel restaurant waitress and now my admin, crying in a cubicle just outside of my office. She started the job a week ago, but I have not seen her since the Saturday before that. She saw me and turned away in disgust.

"What's wrong, Stephanie?" I asked, confused.

"How could you?" she said without turning toward me.

"How could I what? What's going on?"

She swung the chair around and seemed angry now. "They fired me! You said you had a better job for me and now I don't have a job at all."

"I don't understand," I said genuinely. "What is happening here? Why are they letting you go?"

"I don't know," she replied, wiping her tears away. "I just got an email this morning that they're letting go of all the contract employees and interns and then an HR lady showed up with a box and told me I have an hour to pack things up and leave."

I felt my face flush with anger. I threw my laptop bag into my office and rushed to Jim Miller's office. He was sitting at his desk staring blankly out the window when I walked in.

"What the hell is going on, Jim!" I demanded as I stood over him. He looked at me calmly, but did not answer. "Why are you letting people go? We still have a shot to win the Volta business."

"It's not me. It's the CEO's decision and he has the right to do that," he finally replied.

"What in the world do you mean?" I said, confused.

"Bill Rasor is the CEO and he felt that he needed to cut cost in order to meet his numbers."

"What numbers? What are you talking about?"

Jim turned to stare at the window again, apparently not wanting to face me, and said, "This is between you and me, but Rasor's contract runs out in three months. If we fire him now, his golden parachute would kick in and the board didn't want to spend another five million. So, we agreed to keep him until his contract expires and let him do what he needs to do in order to meet his budget numbers which triggers his bonus."

I stared at him for a moment trying to process the information. This was unbelievable. Did anyone think about the people that are being kicked out of the building? While these guys are playing corporate politics, people are going home to face their families and the prospects of trying to make ends meet without their jobs.

"This is the most screwed up company that I've ever worked for," I finally said angrily. "Why did you bring me here? I didn't want to come here in the first place and then you made me stay here when I wanted to leave. Now this. Why?!"

Just then we heard a knock on the door. We both turned and saw Emily standing in the doorway with a cardboard box in her hands.

"Sorry for interrupting," she said, "I just wanted to say good bye."

"Emily?" is the only thing that came out of my mouth. I was shocked and felt horror come over my face. I had no idea that she was a contract employee.

"It was a pleasure to work for both of you," she replied calmly. "I wish you both the best of luck. I hope you're successful in turning Electronica around."

"I don't understand…" I tried to say.

"And Doug, I think it would be best if you didn't call me," she interrupted me.

"Thank you, Emily. You're the best," said Jim for both of us and she walked out, maybe forever out of my life.

Jim stood up and walked around his desk to put his arm around my shoulders. "I'm sorry, Doug. I didn't mean for it to go this way."

"You said his contract expires in three months. Who will be the new CEO?" I asked.

"The board hasn't decided yet," said Jim with hesitation.

I looked at him suspiciously, because I had a bad feeling. "It's Meadows, isn't it?"

"The board is split, but he's one of the candidates, yes," he admitted.

I shook my head in disgust and stormed out.

***

I sat in my office for a while trying to comprehend the situation and determine what to do next. My first reaction was to walk back into Jim's office and quit, but then I thought about all the people that I would be abandoning, including Jim. If we do not win this Volta business, more people would lose their jobs. I thought about all the engineers that were in the cost reduction workshop and all the nice people that we met at the manufacturing plant and even the scary Melissa Connors in Purchasing. Maybe even Evan would lose his job. Poor Alex was probably already gone also. I got up and walked over to his cube, which was empty.

"He was let go," said Evan as he came up behind me.

"What did he say?" I asked.

"You know Alex, he didn't say much."

I nodded in agreement. That sounded like Alex, he would not say much. I am sure he was not happy, though.

"I have the updated business case for you, Doug," said Evan and handed me a piece of paper (see Table 4.1).

I stared at the piece of paper for a moment without seeing anything, but then my brain kicked back on, and I decided to stay at Electronica.

"It looks good," I said finally.

"Our BOM cost is down to $82.28 compared to $90.50 before," said Evan. "We lost annual price reductions on a portion of that, but overall, we are still way better off.

"Also, I updated our manufacturing and SG&A costs to the amounts that we'll need on a marginal basis, which saved us another $12.69. I think that will be an interesting discussion with the executive staff, I don't know if they will understand it.

"Finally, the plant was able to figure out a way to refurbish the existing assembly line and the investment was reduced by two million dollars."

"What about the design changes from the workshop and the suppliers?" I asked.

Evan shook his head. "Meadows killed them all. He refuses to change the design."

"What?" I said, shocked. Evan just shrugged his shoulders, indicating he was not surprised. Maybe I should not be surprised either. Meadows has done nothing to help us so far. It was all just a political game to him and he did not want me or Jim to win. He would probably rather lose the Volta business and more people to lose their jobs than let us have a win.

"The business case is still outstanding," I said. "It gives us an insanely good IRR of 137% and about twenty million in cash for three million in investment. The investors will be very happy with that kind of return."

"What do you want to do?" asked Evan.

Table 4.1 Updated Volta business case

Inflation / (Deflation)	Volume ('000)	Year 1 500	Year 2 1,000	Year 3 1,000	Year 4 1,000	Year 5 500		
3%	Raw Material	1.20	1.24	1.27	1.31	1.35		
0%	Purchased Parts	27.17	27.17	27.17	27.17	27.17		
-3%	Purchased Parts	55.11	53.46	51.85	50.30	48.79		
3%	Labor	0.56	0.58	0.59	0.61	0.63		
3%	Mfg. Overhead	1.25	1.29	1.33	1.37	1.41		
	New Investment	0.75	0.75	0.75	0.75	0.75	$3,000	total ('000)
	Cost of Capital	0.17	0.17	0.17	0.17	0.17	$675	total ('000)
2%	Scrap	1.18	1.15	1.12	1.09	1.06		
	Total Mfg. Cost	87.39	85.80	84.25	82.77	81.33		
	SGA	3.00	1.50	1.50	1.50	3.00		
	SGA ('000)	$1,500	$1,500	$1,500	$1,500	$1,500	$7,500	total ('000)
	% SGA	3.0%	1.5%	1.6%	1.6%	3.4%	2.0%	lifetime
	Packaging	0.50	0.50	0.50	0.50	0.50		
	Ship/Other	1.25	1.25	1.25	1.25	1.25		
	Profit	7.86	7.95	6.59	5.25	2.45		
	% Profit	7.9%	8.2%	7.0%	5.8%	2.8%	6.6%	lifetime
	Profit ('000)	$3,930	$7,955	$6,586	$5,252	$1,226	$24,949	total ('000)
-3%	Price	100.00	97.00	94.09	91.27	88.53		
	Revenue ('000)	$50,000	$97,000	$94,090	$91,267	$44,265	$376,622	total ('000)
Year	0	1	2	3	4	5		
Cash flow	($3,000)	$3,126	$6,318	$5,360	$4,426	$1,233		
IRR	137%							
Payback	1.00	years						
5	years of depreciation							
9%	borrowing interest rate							
$675	total ('000)							
30%	tax rate							

"Set up a meeting with the executives," I said with confidence. "Let's run it by them and then quote this thing to Volta."

Tuesday, Day 23 of 28

The executive conference room was packed again with the designer suits. Rasor and his whole staff were there, as well as Jim. The only person missing was Ricardo Rodriguez, who apparently quit the day before. I was told by Jim that Rodriguez did not believe in the new performance objectives and was not happy that we went ahead and took out upfront payments and annual price reductions from the supplier offers on the Volta program. I guess I understood his perspective, considering his whole career was based on achieving annual saving targets, but this was about Electronica's success, not about Rodriguez achieving his objectives and getting a big bonus.

"I looked at your quote last night and it doesn't make any sense," said Rasor after everyone settled in their chairs.

I snapped to attention in my chair. I did not expect a lot of resistance to the new numbers, but I guess Rasor was still in charge and not missing any opportunities to impose his ego. Perhaps, he also wanted to make sure we failed so that the company's continued failure would make his tenure look less bad. Who cares about people losing jobs as long as his ego was preserved?

"Why do you say that?" I asked.

"Where do I start? For one, your BOM cost is down, but you lost the givebacks and the upfront payments we would have received this year."

The loss of that upfront money probably stung him the most because it hurt his chances of meeting the budget and getting that big bonus.

"The upfront payment and annual givebacks are just fool's gold," I replied. "The suppliers admitted that they had no choice but to build those into the first year price, so we were paying artificially higher prices because of it. Basically, what you were doing is taking high interest loans from suppliers and then paying them back in piece price.

"Also, what didn't help us is that we never challenged their price levels in the first place, so prices were already high before amortization of the payments. Our purchasing team just went off of historical price points and assumed that those were appropriate. We ignored our cost estimators who were telling us that we are way off. Of course, having high price points only helps purchasing achieve those annual savings goals, so it was not exactly in their best interest to push the price points down."

"It's nice of you to blame the person that's not in the room," Rasor accused me sarcastically.

"I know that Rodriguez is not here to defend himself, but honestly it's not his fault. His job was to meet the objectives that the company assigned to him and his team. And he did that very well. He was put into a system and worked within the system to achieve his objectives. I can't blame him for that."

"The objectives have been changed," said Jim. "In fact, most of our objectives have changed, but it was the right thing to do for the company."

"What about your insanely low overhead costs?" Rasor continued. "Million and a quarter for manufacturing overhead and million and a half for SG&A? That's ridiculous! How do you go from sixteen million to that? Not to mention that you are down to 11% in gross margin versus 16% that we had before and 18% that our board is demanding."

"Actually, you were way overstating your overhead cost. We looked at the full picture and the overhead costs that we are assuming now are all you need to run this business," I said and projected a summary on the screen (see Table 4.2).

Table 4.2 *P&L with Volta business*

	Brakes - current		Appliance - current		Total - current		Volta business		Total - combined		Brakes - combined	
Sales	$135,000,000		$167,000,000		$302,000,000		$100,000,000		$402,000,000		$235,000,000	
Material	$110,100,000	81.6%	$124,640,000	74.6%	$234,740,000	77.7%	$82,280,000	82.3%	$317,020,000	78.9%	$192,380,000	81.9%
Labor	$1,120,000	0.8%	$1,680,000	1.0%	$2,800,000	0.9%	$560,000	0.6%	$3,360,000	0.8%	$1,680,000	0.7%
Overhead	$4,170,000	3.1%	$9,730,000	5.8%	$13,900,000	4.6%	$1,205,000	1.2%	$15,105,000	3.8%	$5,375,000	2.3%
Depreciation	$2,080,000	1.5%	$2,080,000	1.2%	$4,160,000	1.4%	$500,000	0.5%	$4,660,000	1.2%	$2,580,000	1.1%
SG&A	$11,500,000	8.5%	$18,700,000	11.2%	$30,200,000	10.0%	$1,500,000	1.5%	$31,700,000	7.9%	$13,000,000	5.5%
Profit	$6,030,000	4.5%	$10,170,000	6.1%	$16,200,000	5.4%	$13,955,000	14.0%	$30,155,000	7.5%	$19,985,000	8.5%

"In fact," I continued, "your gross margin for the brakes business improves from 13% to 14%."

"Wait," interrupted George Sewell, the VP of Finance, "why are you showing 4.5% profit for Brakes currently? We're only making 2%."

"Oh, right. 2% was incorrect," I said.

"What do you mean incorrect," challenged Sewell, taking it personally.

"Well, the plant was distributing overhead cost based on labor cost, which skewed the cost toward the brakes business, where in reality, 70% of the overhead cost is due to the appliance business because of its low volume, high mix nature. We store and manage a lot more for the appliance business than we do for the brakes business."

"So you're saying that the appliance is not at 18% gross margin?" asked Rasor, puzzled.

"No, it's closer to 17% gross margin and about 6% profit. You do a lot for your appliance customers that you don't charge them for, so I suggest increasing prices, if possible, or finding ways to make your operation more efficient. The uptime for that part of the business is only 50%."

"I agree," announced Bud Kulig, the VP of Operations, and had Rasor and others swing their chairs toward him in surprise. "Doug really opened my eyes down there. We're already doing some things to improve the situation."

"Thank you, Bud," I said, pleased that I finally had someone on my side.

"Does that make sense to you?" asked Rasor to Sewell who was nervously shuffling papers in front of him.

"It makes a lot of sense to me," announced Jim. "We already have forty four million in overhead today, why would we need another sixteen to add with this business. We're not going to hire any more salaried people at the plant or here, we're not going to expand the buildings, and we're not going to expand our fixed cost at all. All we'll need is to add some variable overhead like electricity and line supervisors."

"Sounds like you're saying that we were too fat before, so I'm glad we cut some of it off," stated Rasor.

Jim saw me open my mouth to respond and jumped in before I could say anything. "Great! It sounds like we are all in agreement then?" He waited to see people nod in agreement, some more enthusiastically than others. "Perfect. Let's go ahead and quote it."

Wednesday, Day 24 of 28

I was optimistic about Volta's response to our offer, but that optimism did not last very long. Pete Jones, the VP of Sales, walked into my office on Wednesday afternoon and announced that Volta's cost estimators crunched their numbers and their target is now $90.

I threw my hands up in disgust and spun around in my chair. "This is ridiculous," I said. "I thought that $100 was what you said would win us the business?"

"That's what I thought," he admitted. "Now Volta purchasing is telling me that they got quotes in the ninety range, which they think validates their cost estimator's target."

"At $90 price, our financials go to crap and we already squeezed the cost to the max. Do you think they would source someone else if we stayed at $100?"

"I'm guessing the low quote is from one of the new Chinese guys and Volta would prefer not to take the risk of sourcing a new supplier or to take on the long supply chain," said Jones. "But, their director of purchasing really listens to their cost estimator, so unless we convince the cost estimator that our price is right, they will feel like we're scamming them."

"Can you convince the cost estimator?" I asked.

"This guy is really good with numbers and usually runs circles around my guys. Do you think you can help us with him?" answered Jones with a question.

I loved challenges, so I nodded my head in agreement. "Set it up," I replied.

Friday, Day 26 of 28

The meeting at Volta was set up for 10 AM that Friday, but as I sat in the hotel restaurant that morning, my thoughts were nowhere close to the negotiation that was to take place, but rather with Emily. I left her voice messages every day since I last saw her on Monday, but she has not returned my phone calls. Stephanie was not here to cheer me up either. Omar greeted me at the restaurant, without a smile this time, but another young waitress brought me my orange juice. I politely reminded her that I also drink coffee for breakfast, but she never came back with it.

I felt like such a failure. I used to think that the failure of my first marriage was not all my fault, but after failing Emily, and Stephanie, and Alex, and probably others, I was starting to think that maybe it was me and me only who was at fault. I hardly wanted to show my face in public and avoided eye contact with others in the restaurant to make sure nobody else got caught in my trap of failures. Nevertheless, all I could do now is to try and fix this mess.

The Volta headquarters were a giant office building the size of a football stadium. Evan Kaminski was with me in the car as we drove up, and he seemed intimidated by the structure. Pete Jones, who drove us, and his sales rep, Jason Sanders, a jolly old fella, tried to relax Evan with funny sales stories, but Evan did not seem to be paying attention. We had to park what felt like a mile away and the walk to the front lobby felt like sheep going to slaughter. Perhaps, this was all by design, the customer trying to intimidate its suppliers.

"Don't worry," said Sanders to Evan. "This isn't my first rodeo. If you fall off the bull, you'll have three clowns to jump in and save you." He laughed at his own joke and slapped Evan on the back.

"I'm fine," Evan assured us, although his voice could not have been any meeker.

The lobby was a giant open space the size of an auditorium built out of marble and glass. There were at least 50 other people waiting in the lobby, all wearing suits, like us. We signed in with one of three receptionists who also asked us to put stickers over our cell phone cameras. This was apparently to prevent us from taking any pictures of new car concepts or technology while we were inside the building. If Evan felt intimidated before, he was now completely overwhelmed and did not say a word the whole time we waited in the lobby.

"Hello, Pete," said a young man as he approached us. He was wearing casual business clothing that seemed way too relaxed compared to everyone else in the lobby. "I'm happy you guys were able to meet us on such a short notice."

Pete introduced us to the young man, whose name was Felix Ferguson and who was the lead braking commodity buyer. We chitchatted about various mundane things as we traversed many hallways and elevators for what it seemed like another mile until we arrived at a small conference room. There, another man was already waiting for us.

"Hi, Chuck," said Sanders to the man. "I'm surprised you're here this late on a Friday." He laughed at his joke and slapped the man on the back.

"It's not hunting season yet, so I'm here," said Chuck with a smirk.

Evan and I introduced ourselves to Chuck, who was a tall man with large hands, and who seemed a better fit on a factory floor than in this large palace of an office building. Just like many other men who I met in manufacturing, he was secure in his position and ready to rumble.

"It is nice meeting you, Chuck," I said trying to soften him up. "Jason mentioned that you came up from a tool and die shop. That's a great background to have in your current job."

"Thanks," he replied, "it's good to understand manufacturing when you're estimating manufacturing cost."

"Indeed," I agreed. "I assume then that you had a chance to analyze our cost breakdown?"

"Yes, I sure did," he said and asked the Volta buyer, Felix, to project it on the screen (see Table 4.3). "I think we have a lot to discuss."

Table 4.3 Brake system CBD for Volta

COST ESTIMATE - BREAKDOWN SHEET

Supplier Name: Electronica
Program(s): Volta FSA79
Part Number: NA
Part Description: Braking system
Additional Information:
Prepared by: Evan Kaminski

Date: NA
RFQ Number: NA
ECN #:

Total Volume: 10,00,000
Supplier Mfg. Location: USA
Supplier Shipping Location: USA
Currency: Dollar
Exchange Rate:

Yellow Cells are for Input
Blue Cells are for Output Results

A) RAW MATERIAL:

RAW MATERIAL COST

MATERIAL DESCRIPTION	Raw Material Stock Size (LxWxTH)	Gross Material Weight	Net Material Weight	Unit of Measure	Cost/Unit	Gross Raw Material Cost (/pc)
Sealant		0.9136	0.8125	kg	$73.00	$73.00
Solder		0.9580	0.9490	kg	$5.00	$0.2500
					TOTALS	$1.1990

ENGINEERED SCRAP

Eng. Scrap Weight	Gross Raw Material Cost (/pc)M	Eng. Scrap Material Cost (/pc)	Eng. Scrap Resale Cost/Unit	Eng. Scrap Credit (/pc)
0.0910	$0.9490	$0.0000	$0.0000	$0.0000
0.0100	$0.2500	$0.0000	$0.0000	$0.0000
	TOTALS	$1.1990	TOTALS	$0.0000

TOTAL

Total Raw Material Cost
$0.9490
$0.2500
$1.1990

B) PURCHASED COMPONENTS & MATERIAL:

PURCHASED MATERIAL COSTS

ITEM DESCRIPTION	Supplier Name	Number of Unit(s)	Unit of Measure	Cost/Unit
ECU Housing		1		$15.6800
AL Block		1		$7.9500
Connector		1		$3.5000
Other - Electronic		1		$35.1200
Other - Mechanical		1		$19.9500
			TOTALS	

TOTAL

Purchased Materials
$15.6800
$7.9500
$3.5000
$35.1200
$19.9500
$82.2000

C) PROCESS COSTS:

PROCESS TIME PER PIECE

PROCESS DESCRIPTION	Pure Cycle Time (sec)	Utilization(%)	Pieces Per Cycle	Standard In/pc	Labor Standard In/pc
SMT	18.0	80%	1	0.0060	0.0060
Final Assembly	18.0	80%	1	0.0040	0.0200

DIRECT LABOR COST

No. Of Operations	Base Labour Rate ($/hr)	Labour Cost ($)
2	$25.00	$0.2900
5	$25.00	$0.5000
	TOTALS	$0.7900

OVERHEADS

Hourly OH Rate ($/hr)	OH Cost ($)
$264.00	$1.0140
$345.00	$1.9800
TOTALS	$2.3960

CAPITAL

Hourly Depreciation Rate ($/hr)	Depreciation Cost ($)
$58.00	$0.2360
$46.00	$0.2640
TOTALS	$0.6000

TOTAL COST

Total Labour & OH Cost
$1.4520
$2.1440
$3.8960

D) LOGISTICS, PACKAGING & AMORTISATION:

Cost Type	Description	Cost / Piece
FREIGHT	Cost % 1.0%	$0.6788
PACKAGING	Cost % 0.5%	$0.4304
DUTY & WAREHOUSE	Cost % 0.5%	$0.4304
TOOLING AMORTISATION	Interest % 10.0%	$0.1319
TOOLING B&R	Cost % 0.2%	$0.1742
	TOTALS	2.0474

TOTAL COST

MANUFACTURING COST (A+B+C)		$87.9799
FREIGHT, PACK, AMORTISATIONS		$2.0474
	Scrap: 2.0%	$1.7415
	SG&A: 6.6%	$5.2248
	Profit %: 4.0%	$3.6250
TARGET PRICE		**$99.5714**

% of Total

RAW MATERIAL	1.1%
PURCHASED PARTS	82.6%
LABOUR & OVERHEAD	3.6%
SCRAP	1.7%
AMORTISATION	0.1%
LOGISTICS & PACKAGING	1.7%
SG&A	5.2%
PROFIT	3.5%

COST PARETO CHART (% of total)

"I agree," I threw out, "and I'm sure you will agree also with the points we have to present."

"Not unless you have a price reduction to propose," he replied sternly. "Your BOM cost is way too high and so are your overhead rates. I hope you have an explanation for that."

"Well, we never got your estimate, so I don't know what you mean by 'way too high'," I said. "Can you first explain what you estimate those costs to be?" This was a deliberate tactic to get him to explain his numbers instead of us trying to explain ours.

He looked at me with irritation and said, "I estimate your price should be at $90."

"I understand, but what do you think the overhead rates should be?" I asked as pleasantly as I possibly could. Evan and I have artificially increased the overhead rates to hide profit. I chose the overhead rates for this because I knew that these were the most difficult for customer cost estimators to prove wrong.

"They should be at least half of what you showed," said Chuck reluctantly.

"Wow!" I exclaimed. "That's much lower than what we have at our plant. How did you calculate your rates?"

"We have cost estimating software that tells us the rates," he said with increasing irritation and hoping that a mention of software will shut me up.

"I hope you understand that cutting the rates in half will give us only $1.20 per piece, which is only about $1,200,000 per year to cover all the overhead required to run this part?" I stated and watched him get lost for words. "And that's in the three years of full production. In the ramp up and ramp down years, this is only $600,000 and we have to spend just as much to start up production. We have to buy your equipment one year in advance and hire and train a crew six months in advance. Of course, you'll want parts produced during this time for testing.

"And, this money has to pay for the building rental, all the electricity that's consumed, the manufacturing and quality engineers, the salaried staff that we will have to hire and train the direct employees, the uniforms, the material handlers, the warehouse and its staff, the plant management, the office space for all those people, their laptops and telephones, and on, and on, and on. $1,200,000 would not cover that. In fact, we had to put a task on our manufacturing guys to get them to $2,400,000 per year. They don't quite know yet how they will get there. If you recall, we cut our price from $130 originally to now $99. We're taking on a lot of risk to even assume that we'll get there somehow. Our overhead cost now is five times that of labor and we assumed that we'll cut that down to three and a half that of labor. We'll have a lot of work to do to get there.

"Not to mention that I have to also keep getting better every year in order to keep up with 3% price reductions I have to give you every year. However, I can't make any changes to my manufacturing process without your approval, which also requires me to share the savings with you."

Chuck and everyone else in the room stared at me. "But our Chinese supplier quoted lower overhead rates also," said Chuck weakly.

So there it was, the confirmation that it was that Chinese supplier trying to sweep in and win the business. I looked at Chuck straight in the eyes and instinctively pushed on.

"If I was them, I would do that also," I said. "I'm sure these guys want to get their foot in the door. However, what you will get from them and you will not get from us is risk. First of all, their overhead rates are probably lower because the labor in China is a quarter of the cost here in the United States, but let's be honest, these guys have never made a braking system for you. Their cost does not account for thousands and maybe millions of dollars that you'll spend on you and your design engineers, and your quality engineers, and tooling engineers flying over there and spending thousands of hours teaching them how to make products to your high standards. Their cost probably also doesn't include millions of dollars of product that you'll have to scrap every time you make a design change because they have four weeks of product on the ocean and a bunch more in warehouses at any given time. Not to mention all the freight costs and tariffs that may or may not be there when you launch. Believe me, that's all going to come out of Volta's pocket.

"In the meantime, Electronica is here in the USA and have been making braking systems for decades. Our engineering is best in class and so is our quality, so you and your buyer and your quality engineer will never have to be bothered with saving us from another quality spill or warranty recall. Our rates are higher, but you will not have to put up with all the other hidden costs that you would with this Chinese supplier."

Felix turned to Chuck hoping that his cost estimator will have a good answer, but none came out. "So, maybe we're ok with your overhead cost. Is there anything else, Chuck," he said.

"How about your purchased component costs?" Chuck shot back trying to regain momentum.

"What about them?" I asked innocently.

"Your other electrical and mechanical costs are very high," Chuck pointed out.

This guy knew exactly where our problems were hidden. We never addressed those two cost buckets because we did not have time, and we were still carrying built in annual price reductions in those numbers. However, he would not understand or accept the fact that part of our bill of materials (BOM) cost was inflated because suppliers were building in price reductions into the first year price.

"I agree," I admitted. "We have some work to do there. On electronic components, our volumes are currently too low and the suppliers are not willing to give us lower prices until those volumes increase. However, we're confident that we'll be able to achieve higher volumes with this new business and others that we're targeting, so we expect those prices to go down over time. We already assumed this in our business case. Did you assume it in yours?"

"What do you mean?" asked Chuck, confused.

"Isn't your estimate a business case that takes into account the full program life cost?

"No," he said. "We use today's cost."

"Oh, I see. You're using point in time estimating, basically assuming that the cost reflects today's economics and will stay the same throughout program life." I saw him nod begrudgingly, so I continued, "We actually build business case models that simulate cost assumptions for every year of the program life. We do this, because, unfortunately, the cost doesn't stand still in time. Almost all costs go up over time, including salaries, fringe benefits like healthcare coverage for workers, rent, electricity, gas, freight, pretty much everything. In fact, the program launch is not for another three years and those costs will be going up in the next three years as well as all five years of the program life. We have to account for all that in order to make some profit."

The Volta buyer, Felix, exhaled in frustration when he did not hear a good argument from his cost estimator, then said, "Look, guys, the truth is that I can't source your ten dollars over your competition. My management won't accept it. So, I understand where you're coming from, but I need you to come down on your pricing or we'll have to go with someone else."

Just like that we were done with a data-driven discussion. The rest of the meeting was purely a commercial discussion that our sales guys took care of, and it was just like watching two roosters posture for a fight that never happens. The bottom line was that we had to get down to 90 U.S. dollars price regardless of what our cost was, and we had to come up with it by Wednesday. It was nothing new in the cutthroat corporate world that things came down to the lowest price, but it was unfortunate that the customer did not care about any other circumstances or their own costs outside what they paid in piece price. I suspected that Volta purchasing had very similar performance objectives to what Electronica used to have, very much focused on annual savings and nothing else.

"Good job, Doug!" said Pete Jones as we walked back to our car. "I've never seen anyone shut Chuck up before."

"Thanks," I replied. "We still have a ten dollar problem."

"Your arguments were completely opposite of what we did with our plant and suppliers last week," Evan spoke up for the first time since we arrived at Volta and he seemed astonished.

"Every negotiation is separate," I said amused, "you have to adjust to your audience and always keep in mind what the objective is and what the other side will challenge."

"But you lied about the overhead and didn't even blink," he said.

I laughed and so did our sales guys. "I wasn't lying, I was negotiating," I replied.

Monday, Day 29 of 28

I spent the weekend playing with our business case trying to find a way to make the Volta program profitable at 90 U.S. dollars, but there was no way to get there with the costs that we had. The only feasible way was to change the design. So, waking up on Monday morning, I was not looking forward to the fight I would have to start with Tim Meadows, the VP of Engineering. He was very stubborn and has not budged at all since I started with Electronica four weeks ago. What was worse, he was a candidate to be the next CEO after Bill Rasor's exit in the next couple of months, so he was not motivated to do anything for anyone. In fact, a failure by the current regime to win the Volta business might be helpful to Meadows in securing the CEO position.

The office felt empty without Emily and Stephanie to greet me as I entered the Electronica building. Maybe it was just in my head, but the atmosphere seemed subdued in general with hardly anyone interacting at the coffee station. It was as if everyone was waiting for the axe to drop. Not the best environment to focus on your work.

I walked straight to the conference room where we were going to meet with other executives to discuss the quote. Evan was already there playing with the business case that was projected on the screen.

"Did you find the magic bullet?" I asked him.

He shook his head. "No," he said simply.

I now noticed that his eyes were red from exhaustion. He must have spent his whole weekend trying to figure this out.

Jim Miller, Tim Meadows, Pete Jones, and Carmen Lee walked into the conference room. Carmen was now the new interim VP of Purchasing, and she seemed to be walking on stilts she was so proud of her accomplishment. Jim asked me last week for a recommendation, and I suggested Carmen. She had a lot to learn, but she was coachable and buying into the idea that there might be better ways of doing business than what she was used to.

I greeted everyone and asked Evan to display the business case with a 90 U.S. dollars price per Volta's demand (see Table. 4.4).

"So, as you know," I said, "Volta dropped a bomb on us on Friday and is now demanding a $90 price. Unfortunately, as you can see on the screen, that destroys our business case completely, we would lose money on this business from the start and it would just get worse. Evan and I have been playing with the numbers all weekend, but our costs are already at the lowest possible level, so I've concluded that the only solution is to incorporate several cost reduction ideas into the design."

"I'm not changing the design," interrupted Meadows.

"Why not?" asked Jim sternly.

Meadows stared at Jim for a moment, and if the two had horns, they might have charged each other at that moment.

"I'm not taking a risk by putting a design out there that might not work," said Meadows.

"If we don't take that risk, then we take the risk of never having a design to launch at all," I butted in.

Table 4.4 Volta business case with 90 U.S. dollars price

Inflation / (Deflation)	Volume ('000)	Year 1 500	Year 2 1,000	Year 3 1,000	Year 4 1,000	Year 5 500		
3%	Raw Material	1.20	1.24	1.27	1.31	1.35		
0%	Purchased Parts	27.17	27.17	27.17	27.17	27.17		
-3%	Purchased Parts	55.11	53.46	51.85	50.30	48.79		
3%	Labor	0.56	0.58	0.59	0.61	0.63		
3%	Mfg. Over-head	1.25	1.29	1.33	1.37	1.41		
	New Investment	0.75	0.75	0.75	0.75	0.75	$3,000	total ('000)
	Cost of Capital	0.17	0.17	0.17	0.17	0.17	$675	total ('000)
2%	Scrap	1.18	1.15	1.12	1.09	1.06		
	Total Mfg. Cost	87.39	85.80	84.25	82.77	81.33		
	SGA	3.00	1.50	1.50	1.50	3.00		
	SGA ('000)	$1,500	$1,500	$1,500	$1,500	$1,500	$7,500	total ('000)
	% SGA	3.3%	1.7%	1.8%	1.8%	3.8%	2.2%	lifetime
	Packaging	0.50	0.50	0.50	0.50	0.50		
	Ship/Other	1.25	1.25	1.25	1.25	1.25		
	Profit	-2.14	-1.75	-2.82	-3.87	-6.40		
	% Profit	-2.4%	-2.0%	-3.3%	-4.7%	-8.0%	-3.8%	lifetime
	Profit ('000)	($1,070)	($1,745)	($2,823)	($3,875)	($3,200)	($12,713)	total ('000)
-3%	Price	90.00	87.30	84.68	82.14	79.68		
	Revenue ('000)	$45,000	$87,300	$84,681	$82,141	$39,838	$338,960	total ('000)
Year	0	1	2	3	4	5		
Cash flow	($3,000)	($374)	($472)	($1,226)	($1,962)	($1,865)		
IRR	#NUM!							
Payback	-	years						
5	years of depreciation							
9%	borrowing interest rate							
$675	total ('000)							
30%	tax rate							

Meadows gave me a nasty stink eye and said, "I'd rather not launch anything than launch a piece of crap."

"You have no choice but to make it work," said Jim.

"And who's going to make me? I don't work for you," spat out Meadows with venom.

Jim paused and stared at Meadows calmly. "Would you guys mind giving Tim and me five minutes?" he finally said to the rest of people in the room. I started to get up with everyone else. "You can stay, Doug." I sat back down as ordered, even though I was not sure that I wanted to witness the rest of this conversation.

"You do work for me," said Jim after everyone left the room. He pushed his phone across the table to Meadows, watched Meadows read for a few seconds, then continued, "Your friend on the board, Robert Sterling, has elected to retire and, last night, the board elected me as the new Chairman of the Board and CEO of Electronica. The business is going back under the Miller family management."

Meadows's face turned into a weird patch of red and pale spots, but he did not say anything. My own face must have flushed red also, because my heart started pumping in angry suspicion of what Jim meant about company going back under Miller family management.

"So," continued Jim, "I am now giving you a directive to incorporate the design changes per the cost reduction workshop and per the feedback we got from suppliers and to develop a final design that will meet all performance and quality requirements. I suggest that you empower your team to be creative and use their talents and skills to the fullest extend and to not constrain them in any way by fear or otherwise."

Meadows still did not say anything but just picked up his things and walked out.

"Miller family?" I asked after a moment.

"Sorry," replied Jim, "I should have told you a long time ago. My family used to own Electronica."

I shook my head in disbelief. That explained why Jim cared so much about this company. "You've got to be kidding me. You hid that from me since college?"

"I apologize, I didn't want you to think that I was some kind of stuck up rich boy."

"Well, it didn't work, I always felt you were stuck up," I spat out teasingly.

Jim burst out laughing, and I did the same.

"Well, I guess congratulations are in order," I said finally.

"Thank you," Jim replied. "The official announcements will come out soon, so please keep it confidential for now."

I nodded in agreement. "Do you think Meadows will leave the company?" I asked hoping that he would.

"I don't think so, he'd lose his royalties on that flipped board design," Jim stated as if it was a well-known fact.

I gasped in horror. "You're paying him royalties?" I said and almost choked on my own words.

He put a finger to his mouth to keep me quiet. "I know, Doug. My father made a lot of mistakes when he took the company over from my grandfather. Meadows is a brilliant engineer and my father thought that he needed to pay him in order to keep him here."

"May we join you again?" asked Pete Jones from the doorway.

Jim waived them back in. "Great news, Tim agreed to incorporate the design changes," he announced as everyone settled back into their chairs. "How much are those worth, Doug?"

"Roughly $3.80 is feasible," I replied and started to update the business case (see Table 4.5), "which is enough to give us a minimal IRR of 23% and about $4.5M in profit on that three million investment, but leaves the program in the red the last couple of years of production. So, if Volta decides to extend the program life or give us the replacement program, even with the amortization falling out, we'd be losing money on this program for all those years."

Table 4.5 Volta business case with 90 U.S. dollars price and design changes incorporated

Inflation / (Deflation)	Volume ('000)	Year 1 500	Year 2 1,000	Year 3 1,000	Year 4 1,000	Year 5 500		
3%	Raw Material	1.20	1.24	1.27	1.31	1.35		
0%	Purchased Parts	25.67	25.67	25.67	25.67	25.67		
-3%	Purchased Parts	52.81	51.23	49.69	48.20	46.75		
3%	Labor	0.56	0.58	0.59	0.61	0.63		
3%	Mfg. Overhead	1.25	1.29	1.33	1.37	1.41		
	New Investment	0.75	0.75	0.75	0.75	0.75	$3,000	total ('000)
	Cost of Capital	0.17	0.17	0.17	0.17	0.17	$675	total ('000)
2%	Scrap	1.13	1.10	1.08	1.05	1.02		
	Total Mfg. Cost	83.54	82.02	80.55	79.12	77.75		
	SGA	3.00	1.50	1.50	1.50	3.00		
	SGA ('000)	$1,500	$1,500	$1,500	$1,500	$1,500	$7,500	total ('000)
	% SGA	3.3%	1.7%	1.8%	1.8%	3.8%	2.2%	lifetime
	Packaging	0.50	0.50	0.50	0.50	0.50		
	Ship/Other	1.25	1.25	1.25	1.25	1.25		
	Profit	1.71	2.03	0.88	-0.23	-2.82		
	% Profit	1.9%	2.3%	1.0%	-0.3%	-3.5%	0.6%	lifetime
	Profit ('000)	$853	$2,030	$884	($234)	($1,412)	$2,122	total ('000)
-3%	Price	90.00	87.30	84.68	82.14	79.68		
	Revenue ('000)	$45,000	$87,300	$84,681	$82,141	$39,838	$338,960	total ('000)
Year	0	1	2	3	4	5		
Cash flow	($3,000)	$972	$2,171	$1,369	$586	($613)		
IRR	23%							
Payback	2.00	years						
5	years of depreciation							
9%	borrowing interest rate							
$675	total ('000)							
30%	tax rate							

"That's not a great business case," said Jim. "If something goes wrong just a little bit, we might lose money on this program and I want us to be in a good position to win the next replacement program as an incumbent."

"I agree," I concurred. "That's why I'd like to suggest that we go with a higher price, somewhere just below $95."

"But that's still five dollars above their target," threw in Pete Jones.

"It's a risk," I admitted, "but you were in that meeting, Pete, and I think we have an advantage of familiarity and location. It might not be something that they can quantify, but I believe they are scared of the risks associated with sourcing that Chinese supplier. And, I believe that fear is worth more than our five dollar premium."

"So, what does our business case look like with that extra five dollars?" asked Jim.

I plugged in the new price to the business case (see Table 4.6).

"That looks much better," stated Jim.

"Yes," I confirmed. "It still leaves us with only 1.8% profit in the last year, but the amortization will fall off if this program is extended."

"Plus, we can probably add margin to the program if Volta is as bad as they have been historically in making design changes," added Jones.

"And I think we can improve our supplier pricing if given more time," said Lee.

Jim smiled, noticing the sudden collaboration. "Well, let's go for it then," he said.

Friday, Day 33 of 28

The week was finally over and, in spite of all that happened at work, all I could think of was Emily. She still has not returned my phone calls, so I decided to visit her in person. Nobody knew where she lived, but I gave Jim a major guilt trip, and he

Table 4.6 Volta business case with 94.89 U.S. dollars price and design changes incorporated

Inflation/ (Deflation)	Volume ('000)	Year 1 500	Year 2 1,000	Year 3 1,000	Year 4 1,000	Year 5 500		
3%	Raw Material	1.20	1.24	1.27	1.31	1.35		
0%	Purchased Parts	25.67	25.67	25.67	25.67	25.67		
-3%	Purchased Parts	52.81	51.23	49.69	48.20	46.75		
3%	Labor	0.56	0.58	0.59	0.61	0.63		
3%	Mfg. Over-head	1.25	1.29	1.33	1.37	1.41		
	New Investment	0.75	0.75	0.75	0.75	0.75	$3,000	total ('000)
	Cost of Capital	0.17	0.17	0.17	0.17	0.17	$675	total ('000)
2%	Scrap	1.13	1.10	1.08	1.05	1.02		
	Total Mfg. Cost	83.54	82.02	80.55	79.12	77.75		
	SGA	3.00	1.50	1.50	1.50	3.00		
	SGA ('000)	$1,500	$1,500	$1,500	$1,500	$1,500	$7,500	total ('000)
	% SGA	3.2%	1.6%	1.7%	1.7%	3.6%	2.1%	lifetime
	Packaging	0.50	0.50	0.50	0.50	0.50		
	Ship/Other	1.25	1.25	1.25	1.25	1.25		
	Profit	6.60	6.77	5.48	4.23	1.51		
	% Profit	7.0%	7.4%	6.1%	4.9%	1.8%	5.7%	lifetime
	Profit ('000)	$3,298	$6,774	$5,485	$4,229	$753	$20,539	total ('000)
-3%	Price	94.89	92.04	89.28	86.60	84.01		
	Revenue ('000)	$47,445	$92,043	$89,282	$86,604	$42,003	$357,377	total ('000)
Year	0	1	2	3	4	5		
Cash flow	($3,000)	$2,684	$5,492	$4,589	$3,711	$902		
IRR	118%							
Payback	1.15	years						
5	years of depreciation							
9%	borrowing interest rate							
$675	total ('000)							
30%	tax rate							

finally pulled her address from the HR file. I was fully aware that showing up at her door unannounced could completely blow up in my face, but my feelings for Emily have grown very strong, and I could not leave things as they were. I put on my best shirt and jumped in the car convinced of my decision.

My confidence began to wane when I arrived at her house. It was a small but well-kept ranch with a wraparound porch in a middle-class neighborhood that has probably seen better days. I sat in my car for a while pondering whether I made the right decision. I suddenly realized that I was a complete interruption in her life. She had established her own life in this little house taking care of her sister's two children, and I was planning to rudely disturb what she has created. I questioned whether I was worthy of jeopardizing her tranquility. "Why not?" I finally said out loud to myself, grabbed the red roses that I picked up on the way, and got out of my car.

I rang the doorbell and heard people yelling at each other to open the door. After a few moments, a lanky teenage boy opened the door and stared at me. I stared back at his befuddled face expecting a voice to come out, but none did. "Is Emily here?" I asked.

"You must be Doug," he replied, and the way he said it told me that I was not welcomed here.

"Yes," I said, startled, "how did you know?"

"She talks about you all the time, and not in a good way. I'm surprised you showed your face around here."

"Sorry," I replied a bit frustrated, "is Emily here?"

He rolled his eyes, turned around, and walked away, leaving the door open. I stood there not quite sure what to do. Then, I saw Emily emerge in the hallway and approach the door.

"Hi, Emily," I said and offered her the flowers. "These are for you."

She paused for a moment to look me over, then took the flowers and said, "How did you find my house?"

"Everyone seems to know where you live," I answered innocently.

"Nobody would tell you where I live," she stated firmly.

"That's true actually."

She grinned at my admission. "What are you doing here, Doug?"

"I just needed you to know that it was true what I said to Jim that day about not wanting to be here, but it's also true that you were the only person that really kept me here. I was kind of lost when I arrived, but I think I found my cause again and I think you helped me find it."

She came out of the house and sat on a small porch bench. "If by cause you mean that foundation you started to help those who were laid off, then thank you very much. It has actually helped a lot."

I sat next to her. "You're welcome, but no, that's not what I meant. I meant the realization that my job is not just an assignment and a fun problem to solve, but it's actually about people, about helping people, and about keeping people employed by growing the company. I realized that this is what really drives me and that this is my cause."

She smiled and smelled the roses. "So, let me ask you something Mr. Doug Benson. Did you calculate the cost of these?"

"Didn't even cross my mind," I said and smiled even though I was lying. I was guesstimating about fifty cents per rose to grow and ship it from whatever country they came from plus the cost of the flower merchant holding, prepping, and selling the flowers, which was probably another twenty-five cents.

She laughed, and I was happy to hear that laugh because it meant that her heart was thawing.

"I heard from Stephanie that Electronica is going to be hiring again," she said with a smirk. "You won that Volta business, didn't you?"

I smiled back. "Yes we did."

One Year Later

It was Sunday morning and time to do it all over again. I was exhausted, but the show must go on. Emily's family was originally from Poland and she insisted on a traditional Polish wedding, which consisted of a three-day affair and an open invite for anyone to join. The church ceremony took place on a Friday afternoon, but after that, it was off to a party in an *upscale* barn, if that is a thing, which I rented for three days. It was the only place that could accommodate such an event at an affordable price. It worked out perfectly, and the wedding was the most amazing thing that had ever happened to me. On top of the fact that I was marrying Emily, who was the love of my life, I was evidently marrying the whole town that came to celebrate. It is difficult to say how many people showed up, but it had to be at least a 1,000, and all of them from Emily's side, either her family or people who somehow knew her from the town or from Electronica. There were hardly 20 people who showed up from my side. I earlier suspected that Emily ran Electronica as an admin, now working for Jim Miller, but I did not realize she also ran the whole town. Everybody knew her, and all had nothing but good things to say about her. I had so many people come up to tell me how lucky I was to have her that it made me feel insecure about myself. The pressure was on to prove to Emily and a 1,000 of her close friends that I was worth having her.

"Are you ready?" I asked Emily as we were about to enter the barn. It was only 11:00 AM, but there were already about 300 people there enjoying the live polka band, food, and drinks. I dared not to think about the cost of all that, I had to suspend my constant analysis of it. The only way I could do that was to pretend that it was all free, that somehow everyone volunteered their services and donated the food and drinks.

Emily smiled and nodded. Her beautiful face looked angelic, and she made me feel like this was just a walk in the park. Geez, I was lucky to have her! We marched into the barn, and the polka band started a new tune to welcome us. Everyone got up from their chairs and cheered us on. What was wrong with these people, I thought. How did they all make it back here this early on Sunday after partying so hard the night before? How did I?

"Congratulations to Doug and Emily!" spoke up Jim Miller through a microphone from somewhere. I now noticed that he was standing with the band on the stage. Jim was my best man, and he has given a speech every day of the wedding so far. He looked like he was ready to give one again, and he began as soon as we sat at our table and kissed to a storm of clinking glass. "This weekend we celebrate the marriage of two people that are very special to me and all of you. But, we also celebrate the success that these two helped bring to Electronica." The crowd howled its approval. "Electronica means a lot to the people in this community and what a change in fortunes we have seen in the last year. Not only did we win the Volta business, but we've won four other programs. Our factories will be full again in a couple of years and people are back to work." The crowd got on their feet and screamed in approval. Jim waited for everyone to sit back down, then continued. "It was not easy, but the key was that we made people care again. It's not about anybody's ego anymore, it's about working as a team and sharing common goals. And, of course, as Doug will tell you, it's about cost." The crowd laughed and so did I and Emily. "To Doug and Emily and to Electronica!" Jim shouted while raising his glass. The crowd followed in unison.

The polka band picked up another tune, and it was back to eating and drinking again. Some people even got on the dance floor and started to dance.

"Thank you, Jim," I said as he sat with us at our table.

"You're welcome and it's my pleasure," he replied and looked into the distance as if he had something to say.

"What is it?" I asked him.

He looked uncertain, but decided to spit it out. "This is probably not the best time, but it's been eating at me all weekend, so let's talk about it."

I glanced at Emily, who looked concerned.

"Is everything okay?" I said, not sure if I wanted to ask.

"It's nothing bad," he reassured us. "In fact, it's good news."

"Great! Let's have it then," I encouraged him.

"Well, I got a call from Volta's CFO. He asked for my permission to hire you, Doug."

My mouth dropped open. I stared at him shocked and lost for words.

"You said no, right?" said Emily.

"I said yes, actually," replied Jim but obviously a bit scared of Emily's reaction. "And let me explain why. I've known Doug a long time and he's always looking for a new challenge. In college, he picked up tennis because I challenged him to it one time and he was beating me within a year. Then, guess what, somebody said that he couldn't make the volleyball team and he was off to practicing volleyball every day until he made the team. He was only a walk on, but still. What I'm saying is that I know you Doug and I know that you will be looking for a new challenge soon and this is a great opportunity for you."

"What do they want of me at Volta?" I said, finally regaining my wits and realizing that the opportunity might be an intriguing challenge.

"That's the kicker. They have grown so fast that they haven't had time to focus on cost and they are struggling to maintain profitability. Their CEO wants to cut ten percent of their cost in the next three years."

Jim was right, this is the type of challenge that I might not be able to resist. I looked over at Emily who looked pained.

"I was kind of getting comfortable at Electronica," I said weakly.

"You know that Evan can take over your role and having you at Volta can be helpful to Electronica," Jim smirked. "Plus, Volta's CFO wants to put you on a three-year retainer at one million dollars per year."

I almost fell out of my chair and grabbed Emily's arm for support. She looked at me and smiled. I knew then that I had her permission. Still, it felt as if I was being forced to choose a new path in life. I really thought that getting hired by Electronica and marrying Emily was the beginning of my golden years of settling down and having some stability. At the same time, I knew that Jim was right about me. My heart was pounding with excitement of this new challenge. I felt like a little boy who gets a new toy for Christmas. Sooner or later, I would not be able to resist jumping on a new opportunity. I was not going to be able to coast into retirement. That was just not like me.

"That sounds interesting," I said finally and smiled back.

Postface

The Cost aims to describe a cost engineering process and expose the many things that can go wrong with it. Although the story and characters are fictional, the events are based on real occurrences. If these seem familiar to the reader, it is probably because they happen on a daily basis across thousands of global companies in many different manufacturing industries. Making money is not always straightforward. Having a great product that people want usually helps, but understanding your own cost is critical to success for most companies. Unfortunately, it is much too often that companies do not understand their own cost, which leads to lost opportunities to win business and to make money. In most severe cases, lack of cost engineering capability or its misuse can lead to failed businesses.

The Cost demonstrates various cost engineering methodologies and tools. Starting with the concepts of cost estimating, which is a necessary navigational tool for a cost engineer, to cost controlling and to various cost optimization tools, such as cost reduction workshop and gap analysis, cost engineering requires a spectrum of activities to assure the lowest possible cost. The cost engineering process requires disciplined control throughout the product development process and throughout the complete lifecycle of a product. Gate reviews during a product's development are common for many companies, but cost optimization efforts should also be part of the process. It is too late to start those activities only after the design is finalized, or worse, after the tools are built. Cost optimization must take place as early as the concept design. It is not enough to build a product that works, it must also cost only as much as the price and profit requirements dictate.

Cost optimization tools such as functional analysis or TRIZ should be employed early and often. These tools help engineers focus on critical functions that their products are required to perform, not on specific components that have been used in the past to assemble into those products. The mindset is very different between the two. Instead of asking "how do I take the cost out of my product?" the question that should be asked is "how can my product perform functions required by my customer at a lower cost?" This is a very different way of thinking and perhaps more challenging, but it opens the door for significant improvements to the design and manufacturing process that are usually required to design original products and to innovate existing products.

Another important cost optimization concept presented in this book is cost based negotiation. Instead of negotiating based on price points, *The Cost* presents a negotiation method that is rooted in facts. Using cost details to negotiate prices with suppliers or customers takes the emotion out of a negotiation. It focuses on bottom-up or should cost estimates and the reasons behind the gap between customer and supplier estimates. This is especially effective when it is a collaborative process between the supplier and customer. The best results can be achieved when the focus is changed from deceiving each other to finding lowest-cost solutions that leave both parties profitable. Ultimately, suppliers are extensions of their customers, and each needs the other just as much, so optimizing cost will be beneficial for both and will improve their partnership.

The cost estimating concepts presented in this book aim to do one thing first and foremost, to keep the cost engineer's mind open to seeing the big picture. Too often, cost engineers choose to follow the established rules and methods that may or may not offer accurate ways of estimating cost. Whether it is allocating cost based on some obsolete method or not considering cost impacts over the program life, cost engineers jeopardize their company's future by refusing to update their methods. There is only one true cost, and most estimates might never be able to get it exactly right, but using the right cost estimating methods, such as activity-based costing or business case analysis, will give a much more accurate result. On the other hand, the wrong estimating methods could send a company on a wild goose chase that could ultimately result in bankruptcy.

It is important to note that cost engineering is not just cost estimating, controlling, and optimization methods. It is also a culture that must be instilled throughout the company's many functions. It is not enough to order a person or a team to use cost engineering. It must be something that every person in the company thinks about on a daily basis. It cannot be something that employees do sometimes, it must be something that they think about every time they design, purchase, and manufacture products. A big part of building the right culture is developing the right objectives and aligning them across the company. Instead of having each function march to the drum of its own beat, all functions should have the same objectives, and optimized cost should be a major part of that directive. The profitable growth should be the number one objective of any for-profit company and all the functions within it.

Cost engineering is also an organization that must be built, trained, and promoted. Whether it is developing quotes or facilitating cost reduction workshops, the required cost engineering skills are very specific. The right talent must be attracted and fostered. Otherwise, it becomes a dead-end job that nobody can be promoted out of or is interested in getting into. Developing a cost engineering capability is no easy task, and effort should be made to develop it. This comes with expansive and detailed training, either internally or outside of the company through organizations such as the Society of Product Cost Engineering and Analytics (SPCEA), which provides cost engineering training and certifications.

The Cost argues that cost engineering is a core function. It is not something that is done only from time to time or is just nice to have capability. It is something that all companies *must* do to be profitable. Engineering your product's cost in such a way that profit is generated requires a cross-functional effort. The term *cost engineering* implies that this is an engineering responsibility, but that is not the case. Engineering holds a key role, as the design is the most important factor in achieving cost targets, but purchasing, manufacturing, finance, and all others are also critical to the success. Cost engineering is an intense effort that could require a dedicated team to manage the process. These would be cost estimators and cost optimization specialist, but perhaps also dedicated engineers to develop lower-cost design alternatives in parallel with the application teams.

Glossary of Terms

BOM: Bill of material, or a list of all the materials used in an assembly.

Cycle time: The time between manufacture of each part; how fast parts come out at the end of its manufacturing process.

ECU: Electronic control unit, or PCBA installed typically in a housing; together with software, the unit controls operation of a mechanical assembly.

FAST diagram: Function analysis system technique (FAST) diagram provides a graphical representation of how product functions are linked or work together.

PCBA: Printed circuit board assembly, or PCB with assembled electronic components.

P&L: Profit and loss statement; describes major revenues and expenses for a plant or other business identity.

Processing time: The time it takes to process each part from the beginning to the end of a manufacturing process.

SG&A: Selling, general, and administrative, or all the costs associated with corporate office and staff.

TAKT time: The time between manufacture of each part that needs to be achieved in order to meet the customer demand.

TRIZ: The Russian acronym for the *theory of inventive problem-solving*, an international system of creative problem-solving developed in the Union of Soviet Socialist Republics (USSR) between 1946 and 1985 by engineer and scientist Genrich S. Altshuller and his colleagues.

VA/VE: Value analysis/value engineering; cost optimization methodology that emphasizes value to the customer as a guide in developing designs.

Recommended Literature

It is a long road to a full understanding of cost engineering methodologies, but the books listed here will make that road easier to travel.

"Activity Based Costing: Making it Work for Small and Mid-Sized Companies" by Douglas T. Hicks

"And Suddenly the Inventor Appeared" by Genrich Altshuller

"Cost Engineering: A Practical Method for Sustainable Profit Generation in Manufacturing" by Chris Domanski

"Lean Thinking: Banish Waste and Create Wealth in Your Corporation" by James P. Womack and Daniel T. Jones

"Lies, Damned Lies, and Accounting: How Capacity Management Enables Improved Cost and Cash Flow Management" by Sr. Reginald Tomas Lee

"Realistic Cost Estimating for Manufacturing" edited by Michael Lembersky

"Switch: How to Change Things When Change Is Hard" by Chip Heath and Dan Heath

"Target Costing and Kaizen Costing" by Yasuhiro Monden

"Target Costing: The Next Frontier in Strategic Cost Management" by Shahid L. Ansari and Jan E. Bell

"Techniques of Value Analysis and Engineering" by Lawrence D. Miles

"The Goal: A Process of Ongoing Improvement" by Eliyahu M. Goldratt

"The Toyota Way: 14 Management Principles from the World's Greatest Manufacturer" by Jeffrey Liker

"Value Stream Mapping for the Process Industries: Creating a Roadmap for Lean Transformation" by Peter L. King and Jennifer S. King

"Value Stream Mapping: How to Visualize Work and Align Leadership for Organizational Transformation" by Karen Martin and Mike Osterling

About the Author

Chris Domanski has over 25 years of experience in Cost Engineering, Purchasing, Finance, and Engineering in the automotive industry, most recently as a Senior Manager of Purchasing and Cost Optimization at Nexteer Automotive. Mr. Domanski has had the fortune of working for many great companies, large and small, such as Ford Motor Company, Continental Automotive, TRW, ZF Group, Methode Electronics, and Nexteer Automotive.

Mr. Domanski had an opportunity to work for both customers and suppliers within the industry, thus sat on both sides of the negotiation table. In his career, he has been responsible for: quoting, where he developed business cases and cost allocation models; cost estimating, where he analyzed over 300 supplier manufacturing plants and their cost structures; and cost optimization, where he was responsible for finding and implementing cost reduction initiatives. This unique experience has given Mr. Domanski an unmatched level of expertise in all areas of the Cost Engineering discipline. He is thankful that he has been able to help many companies become more profitable and thus save and create a lot of jobs. He hopes that he also inspired others to do the same.

Mr. Domanski is also the President and a Board Director of the Society of Product Cost Engineering and Analytics (SPCEA). The objective of this nonprofit organization is to provide educational content and certifications to cost engineers and other functions within the manufacturing industry. To further spread awareness of cost engineering principles, Mr. Domanski also administers a LinkedIn Group for SPCEA with over 5,300 members and is a frequent speaker at the annual Automotive Cost Engineering Conference.

Mr. Domanski graduated with a Bachelor's of Science Degree in Mechanical Engineering from Wayne State University in Detroit, MI, and a Master's Degree in Business Administration with Finance concentration from Oakland University in Rochester Hills, MI. He also holds a certificate in Negotiation and Leadership from Harvard University Law School in Boston, MA.

OTHER TITLES IN THE SUPPLY AND OPERATIONS MANAGEMENT COLLECTION

Joy M. Field, Boston College, Editor

- *The Barn Door is Open* by Serge Alfonse
- *Operations Management in China* by Craig Seidelson
- *Logistics Management* by Tan Miller and Matthew J. Liberatore
- *The Practical Guide to Transforming Your Company* by Daniel Plung and Connie Krull
- *Leading and Managing Strategic Suppliers* by Richard Moxham
- *Moving the Chains* by Domenico LePore
- *The New Age Urban Transportation Systems, Volume II* by Sundaravalli Narayanaswami
- *The New Age Urban Transportation Systems, Volume I* by Sundaravalli Narayanaswami
- *Optimizing the Supply Chain* by Jay E. Fortenberry
- *Sustain: Extending Improvement in the Modern Enterprise* by Scott W. Culberson
- *Managing Using the Diamond Principle* by Mark W. Johnson
- *Insightful Quality, Second Edition* by Victor E. Sower and Frank K. Fair
- *The Global Supply Chain and Risk Management* by Stuart Rosenberg
- *Moving into the Express Lane* by Rick Pay
- *The Effect of Supply Chain Management on Business Performance* by Milan Frankl

Concise and Applied Business Books

The Collection listed above is one of 30 business subject collections that Business Expert Press has grown to make BEP a premiere publisher of print and digital books. Our concise and applied books are for...

- Professionals and Practitioners
- Faculty who adopt our books for courses
- Librarians who know that BEP's Digital Libraries are a unique way to offer students ebooks to download, not restricted with any digital rights management
- Executive Training Course Leaders
- Business Seminar Organizers

Business Expert Press books are for anyone who needs to dig deeper on business ideas, goals, and solutions to everyday problems. Whether one print book, one ebook, or buying a digital library of 110 ebooks, we remain the affordable and smart way to be business smart. For more information, please visit www.businessexpertpress.com, or contact sales@businessexpertpress.com.